ZAUR HASANOV

MAN
OF THE
MOUNTAINS

Translated and edited by
Caroline Walton

London, 2014

In Abdulla Isa's (Zaur Khasanov) novel, the reader is imbued with the fate of its colourful characters. The mystery of the soul becomes apparent and the reader witnesses violence and deceit, cowardice and betrayal, victory and defeat, and, in the end, heroism."

— *National Writer of Kyrgyzstan, Kazat Akmatov*

Using the I-perspective, the main character - a Chechen highlander - shares with us an almost ten-year period of his young life, mainly against the backdrop of two Russian-Chechen wars. With Wahabi influence increasing in his native village, leading to the mysterious death of his father, the main personage is drawn further into his odyssey. Guided by the historical figures of the Azerbaijani poet Nizami Ganjavi and Alexander the Great, Zaur is manoeuvring his future between the ranks of Chechen fighters on the one hand, and taking care of his family on the other hand. Then, a girl enters his life…

—*Matthias van Lohuizen, OSCE Special Monitoring Mission, Netherlands*

As a British poet and critic, I found that Zaur Hasanov's (Abdulla Isa) novel *Man of the Mountains* reached an unexpectedly high plateau of literary attainment. Indeed, this impressive first person narrative immediately caught my attention due to the strength of its "highland" characters. All be they within an exotic, harsh, yet virile, Chechen cultural environment. However, in this surprisingly sophisticated tale of lost innocence and radicalization, it is the terrain itself which acts as the true protagonist. Unarguably, these living, rugged, landscapes gift Isa's "hero" (Zaur) with both an unending courage and naive foolhardiness typical of all those who mature amid titanic panoramas. And as such, this is a genuinely fascinating book worthy of a large international readership.

—*David Parry, Poet and critic (United Kingdom)*

Published in United Kindom
Hertforfshire Press Ltd © 2014

9 Cherry Bank, Chapel Street
Hemel Hempstead, Herts.
HP2 5DE, UK

e-mail: publisher@hertfordshirepress.com
www.hertfordshirepress.com

MAN OF THE MOUNTAINS
by Zaur Hasanov
(*pen name Abdulla Isa*)

Translated and edited by Caroline Walton
Co-Editor Ian Peart
Typeset Aleksandra Vlasova & Allwel Solutions

---

*British Library Catalogue in Publication Data
A catalogue record for this book is available from the British Library
Library of Congress in Publication Data
A catalogue record for this book has been requested*

ISBN 978-0-9930444-5-8

Contents

Prologue

A thin plume of grey smoke rose from the direction of the ruined watchtower in the gorge. Villagers from Dzhariye – 'Gorge of Towers' - which lay on the border with Georgia, were burning corncobs. It was a signal. The convoy was approaching. After about fifteen minutes I had my first sight of an armoured personnel carrier. The reconnaissance vehicle was moving quite fast. Through the telescopic sight of my rifle I watched four soldiers on the vehicle swivel their heads as though scanning the surrounding heights. After another minute or two the main column of trucks appeared, trailed by a thick cloud of dust.

"The Russians have prepared their campaign well" - I thought. The soldiers in the reconnaissance vehicle sat behind armoured protection in case they hit a mine. The vehicle was also laden with sand bags as defence against grenade attacks. But would these be enough? The steep, thickly-forested slopes of the gorge, and the narrow snaking road were ideally suited to an ambush. And the convoy had no air support.

The markings on the left side of my gun sight told me the convoy was about a kilometre away. From this vantage point the road was in full view. We scrambled to our positions and waited for the signal. Waves of heat shot through me. With trembling fingers I wiped away the sweat that dripped into my eyes.

– Turning my head, I saw Al Rashid on my right. He too was highly agitated, nervously glancing across to the other side of the gorge where four grenade throwers and machine-gunners were positioned. Another five stood on our side. I studied him through narrowed eyes. Soon I saw what I had anticipated, as his large, full lips stretched into his distinctive enigmatic smile.

– Everyone check their weapons - the foreigner ordered - God is with us. Today we will succeed; the infidels will get the punishment they deserve.

I was sure that all those who heard his words would feel their spirits lift – everyone was on edge. When the first vehicle appeared in our direct line of fire, the Arab mercenary raised his right arm.

– Grenade launchers, machine gunners and snipers fire first. The rest await my order – his voice was stern.

He had designated machine guns and grenade launchers for long-range attack; assault rifles and light weapons - for short-range combat.

A middle-aged professional soldier in a green beret sat nonchalantly on the personnel carrier leading the convoy. I took a deep breath and prepared to 'take him out.' My instructions were to shoot at officers and soldiers in charge of communication, that is, those who might radio for back up.

– Allahu Akbar! - the Arab mercenary roared, bringing down his arm. In an instant the natural idyll around us exploded.

Grenade launchers fired at the first and last vehicles, which immediately caught fire. I could not make out what had been hit as everything was covered in thick smoke. Cries of "Allahu Akbar" echoed from all sides of the gorge, muffled by explosions and machine-gun fire. Bullets ripped through everything in their path. Bonnets, wheels, canvas covers – trucks blew to pieces in seconds.

"Al Rashid is a military genius" - I had said this to myself many times over.

Using grenades to strike the trucks spoke of his experience fighting against the Russians in Afghanistan. The Ural trucks had thin armour plated sides under their tarpaulin covers which rifle and machine gun fire could not penetrate. Just as I was reflecting on this, two of our men fired grenades at a truck, blowing its sides off. Soldiers spilled out, trying to hide beneath the truck or flatten themselves behind large rocks beside the road. Seeing this, the Arab shouted to the machine gunners to aim at the trucks' fuel tanks. When a tank exploded in the third vehicle, soldiers turned into blazing torches, rolling down the steep slopes of the gorge towards the river.

– Gunners with grenade launchers, attack! Wipe them all out! - roared our commander.

Spurred on by Doku, a pupil of the Arab, our group poured down from the heights to the road. Now the real slaughter began. Soldiers by the river were killed almost at point-blank range. Some threw themselves into the water in the hope that the swift current would carry them away from the ambush. But the gunners could not miss at such a short range and the river soon turned crimson. Corpses were strewn over the banks.

As a sniper I was under orders to remain on the cliff top. Through my binoculars I saw a soldier with slanted eyes – probably a Tartar – who had been wounded in the stomach. He tried to slide under the corpse of a comrade and play dead. But the mercenary's faithful disciples finished him off with their bayonets. One of them plunged a knife into his wound and twisted it 90 degrees. The poor man doubled over in agony.

Unable to look any longer, I swung my binoculars away.

The Arab was walking around the broken bodies, prodding them with the point of his gun, making wisecracks, relishing the details of the operation. Laughing loudly, he posed for photographs in front of the shattered vehicles.

– Habibi! Habibi! - He called to Doku. - You see how God favoured us today! Ever since the great battle of Badr, Allah has always been on the side of his faithful children.

– He is with us at all times, - Doku replied - But it is dangerous to stay here any longer – and we need to get back to camp.

Taking a few more pictures against the background of fresh corpses, and gathering up captured weapons and documents, the group began to retreat along the same path by which they had come. As a result of the attack only two people had survived from the convoy of around fifty: a wounded officer who could barely walk, and a young boy with a charred and shell-shocked face.

We made our way back with difficulty. It is one thing to descend from the mountains, and another to climb, especially with captured weapons. The dense forest was almost impenetrable to light and air, turning the mountainsides into an underworld. The summer heat and humidity made the going particularly hard.

After a minute or so I heard machine gun fire ahead. It was Al Rashid. He had shot the officer. Severely wounded, the Russian had moved too slowly for our commander's liking. Privately I called Al Rashid by a very insulting name - Shaitan.[1] And in truth he bore some resemblance to the real Shaitan in the Quran. The Arab mercenary had been born somewhere between Iraq and the ancient lands of Sham,[2] which according to legend is the birthplace of Satan. Our Shaitan was dark and curly-haired and had lost his right hand. What is more, his eyes glowed as though he was made not from dust like the rest of us, but from fire.

He thought he knew why I was in his band. But he did not know a damn thing. Had he known the truth he would have shot me on the spot ...

This story does not begin today, but ten years ago, a few dozen kilometres from the site of today's operation, in a small mountain village in the south of Chechnya. It was at this time that my father died a tortured death. He died

---

1 Shaitan is an evil spirit in the Quran (translator's note)

2 Sham is an ancient and mythical city in present-day Syria.

slowly and painfully, after witnessing the great war with Russia, family blood feuds, and an armed struggle with radical Islamists. Not only he, but the entire Chechen people were engulfed by these tragic events.

It was in those bloody days that I met an old man who carried me away from the terrible realities of Chechnya. With him, I travelled almost 2,500 years back in time, to the mythical world of Alexander the Great of Macedonia. I witnessed his battles with the zandji[3] in Egypt, Darius in Iraq, with the Slavic tribes of Kantal Rus[4] in Abkhazia, and his search for immortality in Peshawar. All of these legendary travels, wars, ancient peoples and nations have become mirrors of my personal struggle. It was this old man who helped me to know my father, to appreciate the strength of his will, to understand the principles by which he lived and the wisdom of his advice. I do not know whether our acquaintance came about through fate or coincidence ... whatever it was, that old man changed me forever.

---

3 The zandji were literally 'black people,' meaning Africans. Zaur refers to a term used by the great 12th century Azerbaijani poet Nizami Ganjavi (who wrote in Persian)

4 Kantal Rus was the leader of a Slavic tribe

CHAPTER ONE

The Village

My homeland lies in the high snow-capped Caucasus – the region where in ancient times Prometheus sought fire, and Argonauts the Golden Fleece. Here we are still known as *lamroi,* which translates as 'Highlanders' – people of the mountains.

For many years my days began at half past six in the morning when my mother would come to my door, calling softly - "Zaur, get up!" My parents rose at dawn for morning prayers. Before these, they needed warm water for their ablutions. It was my job to bring in wood to build up the fire. In winter I hated these early risings more than anything else. It was so hard to leave my warm bed. But the stern gaze of my father, Abdulaziz, had its effect.

With his face in my mind's eye, I reluctantly got out of bed. Slipping on shoes that had warmed by the stove overnight, I went out into the yard. The sharp cold air banished all remnants of sleep. Gathering up the wood, I returned to the stove. But I could not linger by its heat. I went out again, slithering across the icy yard to the barn. Once I had cleaned out the bull manure I would give the goat's ear a tug to make her leap in annoyance. I hurried to get my routine tasks out of the way so I could go back to bed. I also hungered after the delicious breakfast my mother had prepared for my father.

– Ma, have you put out any sour cream? – I asked. Rustic bread made from coarse-ground wheat flour spread with homemade sour cream was my favourite breakfast.

My mother, who had the beautiful name of Ayna – meaning mirror - smiled and nodded, "Yes."

Unnoticed, I slipped into the kitchen, took a large piece of bread, spread it with cream and, having sated my appetite, went back to bed. My eyes were already closing when I heard a familiar voice. My classmate, Emi, began to recite the azan from the mosque's minaret. "Allahu Akbar, ashadu anla ilakhi illalah" His call to morning prayer warmed my heart as the bed warmed my body. I plunged into other-worldly thoughts, the traditional notes of the azan caught me up and carried me into the heart of a cold and mysterious universe. The world of imagination slipped into the world of dreams and I fell asleep a second time ...

The sun had already risen above the mountains when I got up for school. That year I was finishing the tenth class. My father expected me to study hard so that next year I could go to university in Moscow.

Grabbing my school bag of books, I tried to slip unnoticed out of the house. But no luck. My mother called out to ask if I had taken some food with me. "Yes" I lied and ran into the yard. I would soon be eighteen and my mother still insisted that I take sandwiches with me, to the amusement of my classmates. How could I maintain my cool image that way? And what would the girls in our class think of me? For a young man, these issues were of utmost importance.

In a few minutes I would meet up with my closest friends and classmates - Ruslan and Emi. I hurried up the slope behind our house. Here on the hill, a cold and pure mountain breeze was blowing, as it did almost every morning. In the holy books it is written that in heaven, where the river Al Kawsar flows with crystal clear water, and persimmons and pomegranates grow, a gentle north wind blows. This wind spreads the scent of paradise over an expanse of 500 years. I do not know why the holy books measure distance in years rather than in kilometres. It is not customary to ask too many questions about these books. But it seemed to me that the wind that caressed my face, filling my lungs with fresh air and clearing my mind, was this very same north wind that blew from paradise.

– Take your head out of the clouds and greet your humble servants – said a familiar voice.

7

Emi and Ruslan were standing beside me. The latter removed his sheepskin cap and bowed to me in mock respect like a medieval marquis.

—   Yokels! - I teased them.

—   Come on or we'll get into trouble for being late, - Ruslan muttered.

But Emi and I knew why Ruslan was so eager to get to school. Its main attraction was his first love - Zeynab. They had loved each other for almost three years. With her dazzling white skin, huge almond eyes and long black hair, many boys in school lost their heads over Zeynab. But Ruslan's authority was too great; they all knew that one sly glance in her direction would be asking for trouble. However, few people believed their relationship had any future. Their clans, or as we called them, *teypi,* [5] were hostile to each other. Once upon a time 'a black cat ran between them,' as the Russians say. After long and stormy discussion the council of elders managed to reconcile the warring parties, but a residue of ill-feeling remained. They still regarded each other as Montagues and Capulets.

So Ruslan and Zeynab could do nothing but secretly communicate at every rare opportunity: an exchange of glances, a knock on the classroom window, a thrown note. They could not meet openly. First, because they were too young, and, secondly, our strict customs would not permit an open relationship.

It might have been possible to meet by the river, where the girls go for water. Since ancient times it has been the custom of young couples to meet there. They say that Sheikh Shamil[6] once tried to prohibit girls from going to the

---

5   Teyp – the teyp is akin to a clan and one of the three foundations upon which Chechen society rests, along with adat – tradition – and religion. They teyp system is particularly important during times of war, when a sense of collective responsibility motivates fighters.

6   Sheikh Shamil (1797 – 1871) was an Avar political and religious leader of the Muslim tribes of the Northern Caucasus. For 25 years he led anti-Russian resistance in the Caucasian war of the mid nineteenth century

river, arguing that this practice was contrary to Shariah law. But one of his companions said: "Our youth is founded in this stream, and the love that arises there is as pure as a mountain spring. Our grandparents and their grandparents, too, went to the stream and married for love. For only through true love can a genuine Highlander be born. If you forbid it, real Caucasians will cease to be born, and then who will be left to fight against our enemies? " After that, Shamil was unable to prohibit this practice.

However, the feud between the clans of Ruslan and Zeynab prevented the couple from meeting even by the river. It could cause trouble for Zeynab, and Ruslan did not want her to suffer. But one thing was for sure - Ruslan was hopelessly in love; the idea that his beloved might find someone else was unthinkable.

On the road to school my mind was weighed down by very different thoughts. I was wondering how I would pass the final exams, and still more, the entrance exams in Moscow. With all this on my mind, I scarcely noticed that we had already entered the old wooden one-storey school building and walked into the history class. Reluctantly taking my place, I looked into the sour face of fat Mariam, who shared my desk.

Our history teacher Aïshat Rasulovna told us about the battle between Hannibal and the Roman consuls at Cannae. This battle was one of the highlights of the ancient world. The teacher enthusiastically described how, using military cunning, the fearless Hannibal lured the Romans into a trap, encircling them and driving them further towards the ranks of the Carthaginians. Having destroyed the enemy's flanks, Hannibal was able to surround the last remaining Roman cohorts and wipe them out.

Among the heroes of the ancient world I idolised Hannibal, along with Spartacus and Alexander the Great. I would listen open-mouthed to tales of their deeds. I sometimes think that all the military talent, bravery and heroism of the commanders of the ancient world was absorbed by the peoples of our mountainous land. In fact, most of the heroes of the ancient world passed through the Caucasus. Maybe that's why I see them as mountain men, my kin in thought and spirit.

As I hung onto every word that Aïshat Rasulovna spoke, I threw a glance at Mariam. Her dour expression was out of place in the lively atmosphere of our class.

–   You didn't have enough to eat this morning, sweetheart, judging by the sour look on your face, - I taunted, digging my elbow into her ribs.

–   Shut up! It's no time for your idiotic jokes. Afaq's father died last night.

The news took the wind out of my sails. Everyone knew that Afaq's father had been ill and unable to leave the house.

After school we decided to pay our last respects to the deceased. At three o'clock we filed into Afaq's yard with mournful faces.

We were about to enter the lean-to where the men were sitting, but an unknown boy came up to us and said that we should go into the house and honour the memory of the deceased there. Exchanging glances with Ruslan and Emi, we hesitantly followed the boy. He led us to a room where some of our classmates were already seated. On seeing them we took heart and resumed our inappropriate classroom horseplay. Completely forgetting where we were, Emi and I threw paper balls at the girls and pulled faces at them. They responded in kind. As I bent down to retrieve a piece of paper thrown in my direction I caught sight of an array of pots filled with all kinds of dishes. These had been prepared for guests and were usually served towards the end of funerals.

Nudging Emi in the ribs, I informed him of my discovery. We turned around and began to help ourselves to these delicacies. Ruslan tried to take a stand.

–   It's a sin to steal at a funeral, especially food prepared for guests - he lectured.

– Perhaps God himself decided to reward his faithful servants with these gifts? – said Emi with his mouth full.

– If it is a sin, our whole lives are ahead of us - I said, chewing heartily – there will be plenty of time to atone.

My last words sparked general rejoicing. I saw that Ruslan was vacillating, deciding whether or not to join our 'rebellion.'

Stuffing my mouth with one hand, I managed to fill my school bag with the other. And at that moment Aunt Fatima, Afaq's mother, came into the room. Everyone rose to their feet as she began to greet us one by one. Auntie Fatima had appeared so suddenly that I did not even have time to swallow my mouthful. And so, hastily chewing and hanging my head in shame, I murmured, "May God rest his soul."

Afaq's mother realised what we had been up to and even gave a little smile. But we were deeply ashamed of having disgraced ourselves and turned the mourning into a circus.

– So you should be, you country bumpkins, - said fat Mariam as we left the house.

– We'll have grown wiser by the time we bury you - I promised her.

Having recovered our spirits, we went home.

CHAPTER TWO

Ramadan

It was winter. I was preparing for exams. Already I feared that I would be completely exhausted by May. Problems about trains approaching at different speeds, the number of oxygen and nitrogen molecules in nitrous oxide, the theorems of Thales and Pythagoras, the median bisector, sines and cosines – all these whirled around my head like hamsters in a wheel. I was tired and fed up of it all. There was one consolation – we were approaching the holy month of Ramadan, the month when the Holy Quran was revealed from on high.

This was our month of fasting. They say that in ancient times, when there were no clocks, people simply laid out lengths of white and black sewing thread. If they were able to distinguish the colours then it was too late to eat. It is believed that during this month the angels descend to earth. They say that heaven values good deeds committed during Ramadan a thousand times higher than at other times. Therefore the holy month was the time for making peace, forgiving offences, and throwing great feasts for relatives and neighbours. At the end of Ramadan we celebrated Uraza Bayram[7]. On this day all who could tried to give alms - *sadakat*. As I was preparing for university in Moscow this year, my father decided to honour Allah by slaying the bull.

– Well, where is your animal, I have brought a butcher with me – a loud voice rang though the yard.

It was my mother's brother Uncle Umar, the most jovial man in our village. My mother had four brothers, but my father was friends only with Umar. We used to say that Uncle Umar was a man 'without brakes.' that is he never paid any attention to what he said or about whom. A short man weighing about

---

7   Eid ul Fitr is known as Uraza Bayram in Islamic regions of the former USSR

130 kilos, Umar was notorious as the life and soul of the village; without him no celebration could take place. Everyone liked to discuss my uncle's fantastic appetite. He lifted people's spirits wherever he went.

— Abdulaziz, where is your sacrificial animal? - my uncle repeated.

— Zaur, go and bring the bull out into the yard, - my father asked me.

Hurrying into the barn, I hesitated for a moment before the 150 kilo beast. The bull was chewing something and swishing his tail. Sidling up to him, I stroked him tenderly for the last time. It was very sad that in a few minutes he would have his head cut off. Pulling his rope, I tried to bring him out into the yard. But the bull grew stubborn and refused to leave his stall. I do not know whether he had seen the strangers in the yard, or noticed the big butcher's knife lying on a stone, but the animal stood stock still. I tugged again. Seeing that I could not manage, Uncle Umar and the butcher came to my rescue and forced the powerful bull into the yard.

I have heard it said a hundred times that animals do not understand when they are about to be killed, but something told me that our bull had guessed everything. He knew that his time was up and so he resisted with all his strength. He gave a piteous bellow.

— We'll have to get him on his side - said the butcher.

— Right, - my uncle promptly ordered us to bend down and seize the bull by a hind leg. At the same time he grabbed the animal by the horns and wrenched his neck to the side. Not everyone has the strength to twist the neck of such a powerful animal. In the village there were only a few people who could bring down a bull; one of these was Uncle Umar.

After the bull was brought down we turned his head towards the Kabala. That was the custom – an animal sacrificed to Allah should look towards the Holy

Land. The butcher ran the tip of his thumb along the knife blade a couple of times to check that it was well sharpened. Satisfied, he stroked the bull's flank to calm it down. Then he grabbed its throat and began to recite a ritual prayer: "Bisimillah, Allahu Akbar" and then he pronounced my father's name. This was also part of the ritual. As the butcher bent down to slit the bull's throat, my uncle cried, - Wait! - The butcher raised his head.

— Zaur, run and fetch a glass from the house, - said my uncle.

I dashed into the house without taking off my shoes, grabbed a glass from the kitchen and returned. My uncle went to the animal and placed the glass directly beneath its throat.

— Now cut! - he ordered, and the butcher made three sharp movements across the bull's throat. Blood gushed forth. Uncle Umar's eyes glowed as he watched his cup fill with thick warm blood. Once the cup was full he snatched it up and gulped down the contents. He stroked his pot belly and grunted. To me this was excessive and incomprehensible. It was the first time I had seen him drink the blood of an animal. Among our people this was simply not done.

Then I forgot about my uncle. The poor bull was writhing in its death agony. Thick steam escaping from its lungs poured out of its throat along with the blood. Gradually the animal's resistance weakened. The butcher placed his foot on the bull's neck and pressed down to make the blood flow out faster. Each time he pressed there was an eerie rasp and a fresh gush of blood mixed with warm air from the lungs pumped out of the animal's body. After about ten minutes the bull gave its final wheeze. The butcher waited a few minutes to make sure that all the blood had drained from the bull's body. It had to drain to the last drop, otherwise the meat is considered *haram* - unfit for consumption.

I have heard it said a hundred times that when an animal is slaughtered with a well-sharpened knife it does not suffer. But now, looking at the bull, I was once again convinced that animals experience terrible suffering, and all the stories to the contrary struck me as nonsense.

— When you have flayed the carcass, divide it into three equal parts, - my father ordered the butcher.

The first part was intended for relatives, the second, for neighbours, and only a third would be left for the family itself. To hold a feast when neighbours and relatives cannot afford one is considered a great sin.

I was preparing to leave the yard when I heard Uncle Umar laugh again. This time he was preparing to eat the animal's brains. They are considered a great delicacy. Umar first charred the bull's head on a fire, then he put it in a cauldron and began to circle the fire, waiting for the head to cook. After a few minutes, my uncle dug out one of the eyes with a large knife and swallowed it.

— Eat! Be a man - he offered me the second eye.

The severed eye looked so dreadful that I flinched, drew back and almost lost my balance. Pieces of flesh dangled from it - perhaps nerves and blood vessels. The eye gazed at me balefully, as though begging me not to touch it.

Seeing the horror on my face, Uncle Umar swallowed the eye straight down. He stroked his stomach with his habitual gesture of sated gluttony. If you believe our aksakkals,[8] one of the properties of the brain and eyes of a bull was to increase male potency. But I did not care. In order not to suffer from any more of my uncle's antics I ran off to help my father.

---

8 Aksakkal literally means "white beard", and refers to the male elders, the old and wise of the community. Traditionally an aksakkal was the leader of a village. Acting as advisors or judges, these elders had a role in politics and the justice system in countries and tribes throughout Central Asia and the Caucasus.

CHAPTER THREE

Lezginka

The village was preparing to celebrate Uraza-Bayram. On special occasions like this I put on my Circassian coat, a white shirt and high boots. I slung a belt of bullets around my shoulder and stuck a dagger into my belt. This centuries-old costume symbolised the unity of our people. It graced us during times of festivity and of war.

Accordion notes floating on the wind told me that people were already gathered in the village square. Of all the day's festivities dancing was the most important. However there were other entertainments such as our national martial art – a combat akin to Greco-Roman wrestling. There was also tightrope-walking and volleyball which is very popular with our people. Ruslan, Emi and I hurried along the narrow village streets, eager not to miss a single moment of the coming celebration. As we neared the square the strains of Aksakkal Zalimkhan's accordion resonated through the surrounding streets.

Chechens have dances for every occasion. For us, dance expresses both social standing and the state of our souls. We have the dance of the bridegroom, the dance of the victor, the dance of the aksakkal, where the old man goes into the centre of the square and dances with a stick. It is an amazing sight when a man of maybe 80 steps out with head held high, leaping and twirling with an agility that would be the envy of a much younger man. Among the many types of dance was the lezginka, better known as the unofficial anthem of the peoples of the Caucasus.

– As soon as Zalimkhan gets started I'm jumping into the centre of the square. Let's see who lasts the longest, - I challenged Emi.

– What shall we bet - a bottle of Pepsi? - Emi took the bait.

– Done – I held out my hand.

16

My friend squeezed it. Ruslan said he would be the judge and may the best man win.

In our village a bottle of Pepsi was worth its weight in gold. I remember a few years ago when my father bought me a bottle from the city I was in seventh heaven. Gulping down the contents, I refilled it with spring water and savoured the taste. The water still carried a faint hint of Pepsi. And now I decided to break an arm and a leg in order to try this magical drink once again.

We joined the circle of villagers who stood around the square. The three of us stood in the front row waiting for the next dance to begin.

—   Give us a lezginka, Uncle Zalimkhan! - I cried. The aksakkal took heart and began to play. His fingers were clumsy as they pressed the keys, but the melody lifted my heart.

I leaped into the square as though carried by the wind. Closing my eyes and raising my hands, I traced a small semi-circle with my feet. This rhythmic movement, which I had practised since childhood, was deeply imprinted in my muscles. Stretching my arms wide and snapping my fingers, I faced up to Emi and threw down the challenge my friend had been waiting for.

—   Let's go! - he cried, and sprang into the middle of the dance floor.

To loud applause, we began to circle around each other. As the lezginka gained momentum, the spectators cheered us on to dance ever more passionately.

"Show him that you are a real Highlander, do not disgrace your family, you're a Chechen!" the audience shouted. These words banished all fatigue. With renewed vigour we threw ourselves into the fray.

As I danced the story of our people flashed before my eyes like a film: battles with the Scythians, Arabs, Mongols, and Persians. Our heroes Beibulat Taimiyev - our first diplomat, Sheikh Mansour and Sheikh Shamil who led uprisings against the Russians, the one-legged, one-armed and one-eyed hero Baysanour Benoivsky who fought to the last bullet and fell like a true Highlander. And so many others ...

Chechen dance is a ritual – the collective historical memory of our people. Even if our enemies took away our language and our history it would be enough to perform any highland dance to recall everything once again. When I danced I had the urge to fight, to love, to do great things; only in the dance was I truly in touch with my essence. It produced a state of ecstasy, comparable perhaps to the delight of a first kiss.

We danced for over ten minutes. Aksakkal Zalimkhan and I had reached the limits of our strength. After all, Uncle Zalimkhan was a disabled veteran of the Second World War and could not play for too long. Everyone knew he should have stopped by now. But Emi took no notice, and danced with renewed vigour. This astonished me. Perhaps the Pepsi was no less important for him than for me.

–   Let's put an end to this senseless game - Ruslan grabbed my arm as I passed - I have not danced with Zeynab yet, and the old man's hands are already shaking. If he refuses to play any more I'll kill you both.

Emi also caught on. Ruslan's burning eyes spoke for themselves.

I danced for a couple more seconds and then moved over to the crowd that formed a circle around us. It was enough for the winner to jump for joy, demanding his winnings. But I paid no attention to him. I was covered in sweat and panting for breath. The old man Zalimkhan said he would take a break for half an hour. Meanwhile the little kids threw themselves into an impromptu dance, encouraged by the shouts of adults. They reminded me of ourselves 15 years ago.

–   I have to dance with Zeynab to let everyone in the village knows that she will be mine, - Ruslan repeated for the tenth time.

I whiled away the half hour by arguing with Emi about when he might expect his prize bottle of Pepsi. With the first note of Zalimkhan's accordion we were back in the circle of villagers. Now there would be a Highlander's dance with a girl. Our custom demanded that only one pair should dance at a time. This looked more beautiful. Besides, if there were many couples they might bump into each other and, God forbid, that might trigger a fight. Ruslan was ready and when the first chord struck up, he raised his arms and made a rapid circle around the square. On the second lap, passing by the girls, he stopped in front of Zeynab and invited her to dance. Blushing, Zeynab stepped forward.

The dance proved to everyone how suited the couple were to each other. He was as handsome and virile as a golden eagle, and she was a graceful swan. When the lovebirds' three minutes of bliss were over, Ruslan ran over to us, his eyes aflame.

— Zeynab just told me she is to marry another man. There is only one solution. I have to abduct her.

CHAPTER FOUR

The Abduction of Zeynab

Kidnapping girls is one of the most ancient traditions of the Caucasus. For us Highlanders it is simple. If they won't let you marry the girl you love you have to fight for her to the end. The laws do not prohibit men from abducting girls, but they say that the man must marry the girl immediately afterwards.

Men who marry in this manner are held in high esteem, "Look what he did to win his bride, he fought for his happiness and hers." In the hierarchy of bride kidnappers, the Highlander who abducts her on the very day when she is due to be married against her will takes pride of place. To kidnap one's beloved on this day is akin to stealing the Mona Lisa from the Louvre in broad daylight. There are such brave men amongst us.

After the dance on the Uraz-Bayram holiday we turned into real partisans and literally laid siege to Zeynab's house. Ruslan wanted to know the identity of the pretender to the hand of his beloved. According to our customs a suitor, under the watchful gaze of the bride's relatives, may bring the girl a small gift, such as a pair of earrings. That way we might be able to find out who was is trying to claim her hand. So Emi and I stood guard duty on the street every night while Ruslan tried to speak to Zeynab. But each time he returned unsuccessfully ...

I need her to appoint a time. The rest I will do myself. But she does not even come out into the yard, - Ruslan moaned on the fourth day of the "siege"

Ruslan, it's late. Let's go home, - said Emi, whose eyes were already starting to close – We'll try to contact her again tomorrow. If that does not work, I'll send one of my sisters to see her with whatever message you like.

– Okay, we'll go to bed. But I must speak to her before tomorrow evening – Ruslan insisted.

After we parted to go to our respective homes I had time to consider the reasons underlying Ruslan's determination. I was sure that his love for Zeynab was the main, but not the sole cause. Somewhere deep in his subconscious other powerful motives were hidden. The more I thought about it, the clearer it became that the secret lay in my friend's childhood. They say that one of the Prophet Muhammad's companions once asked him which person deserved the most respect. The Prophet replied: "Your mother." The same man asked: "And after her?" The Prophet repeated, "Your mother." The man asked again: "And then who?" The Prophet said again, "Your mother." And it was only after he asked for the fourth time that the Prophet replied: "Your father."

When Ruslan was only two years old he accidentally fell into the tandoor – the outdoor oven for baking bread.[9] The wood inside was already blazing; the temperature in the oven must have been 300 degrees. Fortunately for Ruslan his fall was broken by a log of wood which had not yet caught fire. In order to steady himself so that he wouldn't tumble into the flames he reached down into the burning embers below to balance on his fingertips. Within seconds the flesh hung off his hand like pieces of meat.

You ask how he got out alive? In our parts kids occasionally fell into tandoors – and sad to say, they usually died. Bur when Ruslan's mother, Auntie Zaira, saw him fall she rushed after him. Ruslan's grandmother, who had come that day to help her daughter bake bread, grabbed Auntie Zaira's sleeve. "It's too late for my grandson," she shouted, "but I will not let you die, too." But Auntie Zaira, pushing her mother aside, jumped into the pit, grabbed Ruslan, threw him out,

---

9   The tandoor is a ceramic vessel about the height of a man whose walls are coated with a thick layer of clay. This vessel is placed in a specially-dug pit. Logs and kindling are piled in. Once the temperature in the tandoor reaches a certain level, women slap dough onto its walls and the bread is baked.

and only then permitted her mother to help her out of the inferno. Her legs were badly burned, and to this day she walks with difficulty.

Ruslan and his mother needed emergency treatment. His father Jamal took them to the best hospital in Grozny, and from there straight to Moscow. In those years almost everyone in the village earned well, therefore there were no problems about paying for medical treatment. Relatives and neighbours helped as much as they could. For four years Ruslan went to Moscow for treatment. Each time, they cut some skin from his buttocks and grafted it on to his fingers. When the treatment was completed, my friend was left with the tips of two fingers missing.

For Ruslan his mother was a saint. Sometimes he would curse his father, and declare that he did not love him even a tenth as much as his mother. In the Caucasus such a saying is unforgivable. But Ruslan's father loved his wife with all his heart, and so he always forgave his son.

And now, as we slowly dispersed to our homes, I realised what Zeynab meant for Ruslan. Thanks to his mother's courage and devotion he respected all women, especially those he loved, therefore he was prepared to go to the ends of the earth for Zeynab.

I tiptoed into my room and instantly fell asleep.

I do not know how long I slept before I was awoken by the crack of a pebble hitting my window. As I opened my eyes, another pebble flew against the glass. I jumped out of bed and went to the window. Ruslan waved up at me. He was holding a pair of horses by the reins.

–   Get dressed and come down as quickly as possible, every second counts - he whispered.

–   What happened? What are the horses for?

– I just saw Zeynab's father and brother taking her away towards the
mountains. They suspect something so they want to hide her. We have to
kidnap her right away –

I tried to object but he interrupted me, saying there was no time to talk, we
needed to mount our horses and chase after them. As I took my saddle, Ruslan
handed me a dagger. "You may need it," – he said, and we rode off toward the
gorge.

It was the first time I had taken part in an abduction. My heart was pounding, a
strange tune played inside my head and my guts were on fire. By now the wind
had turned against us, it blew hard in my face and I felt my ears redden from the
cold. But the chase – the wild thrill of the chase! ....

Ruslan was no less agitated. He told me that after we had dispersed he had
decided to return to Zeynab's house, just in case. His premonition had proved
correct.

– I thought that she might be able to talk to me while all the household slept.
But as I stood against the wall, I heard the squeak of the gate, - Ruslan
stammered as he bounced in his saddle,. - Then I saw Zeynab with her
father and brother sneaking out of the house on horseback, heading for the
gorge. Damn them, they cannot hide her from me!

We spurred on our horses. We had to hurry to reach the gorge, but it was
impossible to ride at a gallop. The road was very steep and narrow. If you lost
control of your horse it could be fatal. As the locals said, "The mountains do
not forgive mistakes." Ruslan assumed that Zeynab was being taken to the
provincial capital where she had family. But she might also be taken to relatives
of the groom – whoever he was.

– You carry along this road, - said my friend, - I'll go up this path and head
them off. That way they'll be surrounded.

— And then?

— I don't know, we'll see. But don't do anything until you hear my signal.

— Please don't lose your head, - I begged him.

But Ruslan swung off up the narrow path without answering. I began to tremble as though I had touched an electric current. If we mess this up they'll cut off our heads. How will this business end? What shall I tell my father? God forbid that blood will be spilled. Then both Ruslan and Zeynab will be cursed for life by their parents and I shall become a mortal enemy of her clan.

At night this road is very dangerous. Wolves are known to attack both animals and humans in these parts. If she sensed a wolf in the distance my horse might bolt. That would be the last thing I needed. I struggled to overcome my fears and involuntary trembling by concentrating on riding.

After 15 minutes I made out the silhouettes of our quarry on the road ahead. They were riding at a slow pace, scarcely exchanging a word. I dismounted, and, leading my horse by the reins, I awaited a signal from Ruslan, with no idea how I would respond.

Ahead of me there was a thud, as though a heavy object had fallen to the ground. A scream came from Zeynab. The figure of her brother jumped off his horse. My horse was badly startled. Clutching my knife, I ran into the thick of the battle. Ruslan had knocked down Zeynab's father and was hitting him in the face. Her brother came up from behind and slashed Ruslan with his horsewhip. As he raised it a second time I grabbed him by the sleeve, tripped him and he fell to the ground. In the darkness the poor youth took me for some kind of evil spirit and began to scream in terror. In an instant the silence of the night turned into an uproar. Everything became jumbled up: my cursing, blows, the anguished screams of her brother, and Zeynab's prayers for help.

Grabbing her brother by the throat, I struck his head against the earth. He lost consciousness. I banged his head again and ran to the aid of Ruslan. Together we tied up Zeynab's father. Ruslan was bleeding from a head wound, but in his excitement he did not seem to notice.

Zeynab pleaded hysterically with us not to hurt her father and brother. She cursed Ruslan and wept. Grabbing her leg, Ruslan pulled her off her horse.

— Don't hurt my father, I'll never forgive you, - she wailed.

To calm her down - otherwise we would not manage to carry her away from the gorge - Ruslan slapped her across the face. She opened her mouth to speak again and received a second blow. She passed out and we put her across Ruslan's horse.

Ruslan jumped up behind her and we rode off in the opposite direction from the village. Before we left I gave our opponents' horses a few kicks to shoo them back the way they had come.

— Where are we going now, Ruslan? - I asked.

— Into the mountains, to the "City of the Dead," I have already prepared everything there - he replied.

— You're crazy. Not on your life!

— Shut up, coward! We'll take shelter in the fortress outside and not in the City itself. No one will ever look for us in that godforsaken place, - he said, as he whipped up his horse.

His words calmed me a little. The last thing I wanted was to go to that accursed spot in the middle of the night. We began to ascend to the place from which in times past no one ever returned, a ghost town built on the bones of our ancestors.

CHAPTER FIVE

Fugitives

What would become of us? The thought tormented me as we climbed up into the mountains. By raising his fists to Zeynab's family Ruslan had overstepped the mark by a long way. In theory we had two options. The first: we would spend the night in the temporary accommodation that Ruslan had prepared and in the morning return to the village to ask for forgiveness from her parents and their blessings for the two lovers. I had little faith in this alternative. The second option was to wait in the mountains for an imam to come and ask Zeynab if she wanted to become Ruslan's wife. This prospect didn't appeal to me at all, nor to Ruslan. But we had little choice.

We left behind us the last traces of civilization, passing isolated farmhouses and huts where shepherds spent summer nights while their flocks grazed in mountain pastures. After several hours we reached a rope-and-plank bridge that hung 20 metres above the surging river Chani-Argun. How would we manage to take Zeynab and the horses over this ramshackle old crossing?

Ruslan did not pause for thought. He jumped off his horse, lifted down the unconscious Zeynab and laid her out on the ground. Telling me to look after her and the horses, he grabbed the rope handrail and stepped onto the bridge. In less than ten seconds his figure had merged into the darkness. Left alone, I began to shiver like a frightened child. I even thought of reviving Zeynab. At least talking to her might help disperse the fear. But damn it, Zeynab did not want to wake up. I sat gripping my dagger and staring into the darkness in the direction of the far side of the bridge, waiting for a sign of life.

Soon a faint glow appeared. It grew brighter until I could discern outlines on the far side of the gorge. My spirits lifted. Ruslan had got a fire burning. He appeared, torch in hand. Heaving the lifeless Zeynab over his left shoulder,

Ruslan edged forward. Fortunately she was a slender girl, weighing no more than 45 kilos. To keep from falling I placed one hand on my friend's right shoulder and with the other I gripped the rope railing.

With slow steps we made our way across the bridge.

— It will be easier from now on - said Ruslan, extinguishing the fire with his boots.

— How far is the fortress from here? We'll die if we have to carry Zeynab much further.

Pronouncing her name aloud had its effect, for Zeynab gave signs of life. I suspected that she had come to a long while ago and had been merely feigning unconsciousness. Anyway, after "waking up", she proudly stood on her two feet and walked beside us. Ruslan made several attempts at conversation but Zeynab would not utter a word. Thus in silence we continued our journey. Dawn was already breaking.

— I can see a tower, - my lungs burned in the thin air. It was an effort to speak;

— Get a move on then, my legs are killing me - Ruslan muttered.

According to our legends, before the advent of Islam mountain people would go up to the City of the Dead when they sensed they were going to die. There they would lie in small caves and await their death. Since then the City of the Dead has had a sinister reputation. Some say that the fortress is haunted by ghosts of the dead, others that the pre-Islamic gods themselves stand guard over their bones.

A stone's throw from the City is a medieval fortress. It is thought that in the middle of the thirteenth century Genghis Khan's troops had their first encounter with the Chechens here. Before that they had already laid waste to neighbouring

Azerbaijan, Daghestan, the Alan capital Magas and eight other ancient states of the region. At the end of their march through Georgia they approached the Argun Gorge, but the fortress stood in their way. Whether the Mongols were exhausted after their previous battles, or whether we put up such determined resistance, I don't know, but after besieging the fortress for a short while, they decided to turn back ....

After a further ten minutes we reached the old fortress, or rather what was left of it. Time had taken its toll. The outer defences had been destroyed, leaving mounds of rubble that were now sprouting with grass. Only the high observation tower stood proudly amidst the remains of former glory. I was surprised to find people living here – the tower was inhabited by an elderly couple who were distantly related to Ruslan.

– We shall find food and a bed with them - he said.

The tower was shaped like an elongated trapezium of the kind I used to draw in geometry class. It consisted of three storeys divided by wooden beams. The third floor was a lookout station. The two lower floors had been adapted for human habitation. We took Zeynab into a small room off the main living area. Despite the cold outside, it was tolerably warm in the tower.

The mistress of the house laid all her meagre supplies on the table: black country bread, goat's cheese and a jug of water. I did not wait for an invitation to eat. Mumbling the traditional "Thank you for your hospitality," I tore off a hunk of bread. Once I had eaten I felt a little calmer. I went over to the wall, lay down and instantly fell asleep. The events of the day had exhausted me both physically and mentally. More than anything else I was in need of deep and refreshing rest. Tomorrow would be time enough to consider the next step.

It was already late in the morning when I rose. My friend was still asleep. I quietly opened the door of the tower and went outside. The wind up here was cold and harsh. I took a deep breath of crisp air. Climbing up the slope, I saw the mouths of the famous caves, the final resting places of our ancestors. Then I looked up into the sky and recalled my home, my mother and father, our orchard, our stable and our streets. I had not been away long, but I already missed them.

– Homesick? – Ruslan suddenly appeared from behind. I felt he had read my thoughts.

– A bit, and this place was not very comfortable to sleep in, - I replied.

Ruffling my hair sympathetically, he added:

– I fell asleep just before dawn. I feel like hell on earth. Zeynab does not want to see my people. She asks only for the imam.

– What did she say to our hostess?

– Why don't you listen when I speak to you? – His voice was sharp - She does not want to see anyone. All she wants is the imam. At once.

– We need to solve this problem fast - I advised.

– Our people are probably already headed for Zeynab's house. God grant that they give us their blessing, - said Ruslan.

But I doubted it. Rather, I believe that yesterday we had started a blood feud. I was sure that the enmity between their families would now turn into open confrontation. After all, we had not just stolen Zeynab, but also attacked her father and brother. This greatly increased our "guilt."

– I'll go down to the village tonight and speak to Emi. He must know everything that's going on - I said.

— I'll go with you, - said Ruslan.

— No, - I answered - Zeynab cannot stay here alone - in addition, we need weapons and food. I don't want to be beholden to your relatives.

Ruslan's face clouded. He patted me on the shoulder and said that breakfast was ready. Apparently our hostess had been signalling to us for the last five minutes but we had our backs turned to her. After breakfast I set off. Crossing the hanging bridge with ease this time, I found our horses tethered where we had left them. After checking my saddle I climbed onto my horse. My heart was pounding.

What awaits me down there? In deep gloom I descended the mountain.

CHAPTER SIX

Scandal

The descent was easier than the way up. The horse behaved well, and I admired the natural world around me. Sometimes when the path became very narrow or steep I dismounted and led the horse by the reins, trying not to slip on the snow which still lay on the ground at these heights. But as I descended I came upon fresh wolf tracks and decided to speed up. Wolves usually hunt in packs and I had only a dagger. It would be no defence against a wolf pack.

Our village lay over the brow of the next hill. I dismounted and cautiously climbed the slope. Looking down, I saw that everything was quiet. There was a light in the yard of our house. I saw my mother there, preparing food in a large pot. They were clearly expecting many guests. I was puzzled - I am not at home, I am on the run, and my family are preparing a feast…

I decided to wait another couple of hours until it got dark.

Jumping up and down and rubbing my hands against the cold, I was hesitating over what to do when the wind carried up some voices from the village. On the road that led from the center of the village to our house i saw my father along with the fathers of Ruslan and Emi, walking with the elders of the village. When they reached our house my father gestured that they should all enter.

As the old men politely removed their shoes and entered our home, I decided it was time to go to Emi's house. I had to ask him what was going on. Keeping close to the low fences of neighboring houses, I hurried towards his house. I was afraid of accidentally bumping into someone. Fortunately, I met no one. I soon reached Emi's window and began throwing stones at it. Emi stuck his head out like a scalded cat.

— Emi it is I, Zaur. Are you alone? - I asked.

— Get in here quickly, you fool, God forbid that anyone should see you. Now Zeynab's whole clan are looking for you - he hissed.

Climbing in through his window, I hugged him. I would never have believed that I could miss this weakling.

— Go on. Tell me everything but without your usual 'ohs' and 'ahs'.

Emi sometimes liked to exaggerate, but I had no time for colourful stories. As I understood it, the situation was serious.

— Yesterday, around five thirty in the morning they surrounded Ruslan's house. They raised such a hue and cry that the whole village woke up. Zeynab's father shouted out that Uncle Jamal must hand over Zeynab and Ruslan. When we went down to Ruslan's gates her brother attacked me. He and several of his relatives grabbed me by the collar and pinned me to the wall. They thought I had been with you and had joined in the attack on them. But my father and neighbours stood up for me. My father had to swear to the holy Quran that I had been at home all evening and never gone outside. Only then did they let me go.

— And my father, was he there? What did they say to him? - I asked anxiously.

— I do not know about your father, but Uncle Jamal cursed his son even more than Zeynab's father did. He declared that he no longer had a son named Ruslan, that he had disgraced him and his mother and that he would kill him before Zeynab's *teyp* did so. Jamal even ordered everyone out of their rooms so that Zeynab's father could search their home.

— And my father, he was there? What did they say to him? - I repeated.

— After searching Ruslan's house, they said they would also check your home. Your father said that the person they were looking for was not in their home. But Zeynab's brother insisted.

– Lousy devil, miserable coward, - I blurted out – he shits his pants when fighting with me, and now he come over the big shot squaring up to my father. I should plunge a dagger straight into his heart so that he will die like a dog!

– Your father said – anyone who enters the gates of my house without permission will be deemed a blood enemy and I will kill him.

The situation grew worse.

– Some members of our clan and our neighbours had already formed a circle around the gate of your home and were quarelling with Zeynab's relatives, when the village aksakkals appeared and demanded an end to this racket. They insisted that all the warring parties should gather together at the home of one of the aksakkals, and there the elders would resolve the dispute according to our customs. The parties to the conflict were made to swear that no one would do anything until tomorrow afternoon.

– And what have they decided, what's the result? - I said.

– I do not know - said Emi - My father has not yet returned. It seems that they are discussing your business into the evening.

– The elders are at our home, my father invited them. I saw them going in half an hour ago, - I said.

– Then you need to wait until they finish the meal, and then I will find out everything from my father, - Emi smiled, his eyes flashing.

– Can I have a nap here? Wake me up when you find out what's happened, okay?

Going over to his bed, I lay down. After a whole day on horseback I was aching in every possible place. I do not know how much time passed until Emi awakened me, but my sleep was calm and deep. If he had not come back I would probably have slept soundly all night.

– Get up, only be quiet, - said my friend, pressing a finger to his lips.

There was some food by the bed: roast meat, bread, salad and water. While I ate in silence, Emi told me what had happened.

– The situation is serious. Today our elders discussed the matter for six hours. Zeynab's family want her back and are seeking vengeance. They said that this is an insult that can only be washed away with blood and that if they do not take revenge they will be considered cowards.

– Yes, well, if it's blood they want they'll have it. We, too, are not going to give up just like that - I said, chewing on some meat and washing it down with a gulp of water. I was still ravenous.

– It's no joking matter; my old man said that passions are boiling over. Ruslan's father brandished a dagger and swore on all he held dear that he would slay his son when he got home - my friend warned.

– And what did my father say? - I asked, wiping my mouth on my shirtsleeve.

– Uncle Abdulaziz said that the young couple loved each other. If that were not so, they would not have taken such a risk. Your old man even recalled a rhyme,

Without love, the corn will not grow as tall as your arm, Only the houses of lovers are quiet and calm.

There was amazement in Emi's voice but the poetic inclinations of my father no longer surprised me. Perhaps his words had astonished everyone. I thought – well, he is old, and when a person ages, he becomes as sentimental as a child.

It cheered me up a bit to hear that my father was calm. This indicated that my parents were not angry at me, at least, not as angry as Jamal was with Ruslan. This in itself it was a great relief. There was hope then, that I might soon return home. With this thought I turned back to Emi, and asked him how the meeting had concluded.

– Without any decision as yet. They talked for a long time, but each party refused to budge. I don't think Zeynab's clan will let it go. They are demanding that the mullah go to their daughter as soon as possible. You need to tell either my parents or yours where Ruslan and Zeynab are hiding.

Thinking about it, I decided Emi was right. I explained how to reach the fugitives. But I asked him to give me time to get there first in order to convey the latest news to Ruslan. In the meantime, I asked my friend to get hold of everything edible that he could find. I also asked him to feed and shelter my horse. My warm "thief's" bed was waiting for me. I had to rest before the morning's journey.

CHAPTER SEVEN

The River of Parting

I awoke before dawn and prepared for the journey. Emi had not only brought me food, but also a hunting rifle. The rifle was old but I was delighted with it. Now we wouldn't have to hide in the mountains like savages armed only with knives. Emi went off to fetch the horse.

Crossing through the garden at the back of the house and jumping over a low fence, I came out into the street. From here my parents' place was clearly visible. Had I been at home I would have already been up, fetching wood for the stove and feeding the animals. "Look at the tricks fate plays," I thought to myself. "Only two months ago I would never have been able to imagine that one day I would miss all the morning tasks that I had loathed since childhood.

My friend returned with the horse. In a few hours I reached the City of the Dead. When he caught sight of me, Ruslan ran joyfully down to meet me, demanding that I tell him everything.

- They are searching for us and they are angry - I said, and told him all that I had seen and heard in the village.

- Ruslan clutched at his hair and began to pace up and down in anxiety.

- Everything will be okay, Zaur. Believe me it'll all be okay, - and added, - there's a cure for everything except death.

As we walked towards the tower I told him that soon, either today or tomorrow, the Imam would come here. He would have to talk to the "prisoner" and then the situation would be decided one way or the other. The prospect of going home soon made us both feel more optimistic, although our consciences troubled us.

I had something to eat and a glass of tea. Then, before going to bed I decided to go outside in order to breathe some fresh air. It was quite cold and very dark. The sky was splendid. Here the stars were nearer and brighter than in our village. They looked like millions of diamonds thrown up by an unseen power, too mysterious for the human mind to fathom. Gazing up into the sky, I thought that there is so much in the world that we cannot explain - black holes in the universe, unidentified flying objects, the secrets of our origins and of the pyramids of Egypt and South America... then I said to myself, forget about the pyramids, we don't even know which came first, the chicken or the egg? And where is the rooster in all this? We are drops in the ocean, specks of dust in the cosmos. Nothing depends on us and we can't influence anything. Thoughts about my own powerlessness scared me so much that I drove them away. I had to stop these fantastic ideas. The more you ponder upon these deep matters, the further you remove yourself from earthly concerns, and one day you might wake up in a rubbish barrel, like Diogenes.

Finally I went to bed, only to be awoken at some time before dawn by Ruslan,

— Someone is coming but I can't see their faces through the mist. Let's go out and set an ambush for them, in case they have come to do us harm.

We slipped out of the door into the courtyard. Rounding the corner of the tower, we stared down towards the gorge. Someone was approaching from that direction. We froze in anticipation. Through the thick early morning mist, which is common at these heights, we could just make out their felt cloaks and large hats which completely hid their faces from our view.

— How did you spot them? - I asked Ruslan.

— I've been on hot coals for two days now, and couldn't sleep. I noticed them by chance when I was looking out.

All the while the strangers climbed slowly but confidently towards the tower. A couple of minutes later they had entered the courtyard. We were straining every nerve like leopards about to pounce on their prey. The strangers were going to knock on the door when we called out - Who's there?

The arrivals turned and together they removed their heavy hats. We couldn't believe our eyes. It was our little Emi. Ruslan threw himself upon him and Emi almost suffocated in his embrace. Our joyful reunion lasted at least five minutes. Emi had brought the Imam with him.

I never thought I would be so happy to see Emi. Ruslan showered him with questions about our parents, relatives, and the situation in our village. I couldn't wait to find out what had happened since I had come back up here.

Emi said that Zeynab's parents were demanding her back, Ruslan's parents were against the marriage, and my family were afraid that Zeynab's relatives would reach us before they did. Our enemies would spread information about us through all the neighbouring villages.

—   To hell with them - I said. - No-one will want to intervene in this business and get innocent blood on their hands. It's a fight between two families, a third would be superfluous.

The imam looked at us disinterestedly. He was not very talkative. In the course of his duties he must have played the role of go-between in many similar situations. Apart from the fact that he had probably never had to climb so high into the mountains, this was just a regular day's work for him. He greeted Ruslan's relative, the owner of the fortress, and went in to see Zeynab. We waited outside. The mullah emerged very quickly.

—   The girl doesn't want to stay here, she asks to go home, I must take her.

—   I'd like to go in and have a word with her, - said Ruslan softly.

The imam returned to Zeynab and got her permission for Ruslan to enter. Judging by my friend's bearing and expression as he went in, he considered himself a doomed man. Fifteen minutes crept by at a snail's pace, then twenty. There was still no news from inside.

"If only he doesn't lose his head and mess things up," I thought to myself. Or, heaven forbid, that Zeynab says something to upset him and he loses his reason altogether. Then all our heads will roll.

— If she rejects him he might kill her, - whispered Emi.

— We can't just stay here and wait. Come on, let's go up to her door. If something happens to one or other of them, then we'll all be held responsible. If we stand outside the girl's door we'll be able to hear what's happening, - I suggested to the imam.

The imam was impressed by my logic, which was actually quite uncharacteristic of me, and we tiptoed towards the door, careful not to make a sound. Luckily, Ruslan's elderly relative was sitting on guard there. Ruslan himself had asked her to stay there and he even left Zeynab's door half open so the old lady could go in if anything seemed untoward.

The minutes continued to creep by. There was hardly a sound from behind the door; barely audible whispers were the only indication of the presence of people in the room.

After another fifteen minutes the door was flung open. A pale Ruslan emerged and told the imam that Zeynab could go home with him. Emi and I could not believe our ears. What did it mean? Had Ruslan given up?

"It can't be all over," I thought.

When Zeynab and the imam were out of sight, Ruslan began to laugh.

— If anything goes wrong, I'll abduct her again, - he said, rather arrogantly.

39

– What do you mean? We're not in a bloody kindergarten where you can kidnap Zeynab every week. It's not a damn conveyor belt. You've completely lost your mind.

As angry as a mad dog, I withdrew into the corner of the room. What the hell was he playing at? He had lost his senses. We still hadn't recovered from the first abduction, and he was planning a second one. And one involving me. I was so shocked, I was ready to punch him in the face. Boiling with rage, I laid my head down on the pillow and somehow managed to fall asleep.

When I opened my eyes, Ruslan was standing by my head.

– I had no choice, Zeynab absolutely refused to have anything to do with me. Only with great difficulty could I persuade her to talk. She was scared to death; she is afraid her father and brother will kill me because I treated them so roughly. So we decided that she should go home, everything will calm down and then we'll try to raise the question of marriage again. But this time with her parents' blessings.

– No-one will give their blessings, not to her nor to you. You had a small but real chance to marry her here, but down there she will be under the power of her parents again.

– She is under the power of Allah, and no-one greater, - shouted Ruslan. - If her parents refuse our request we have arranged how and where to meet and run away again. Zeynab would rather die than marry another man. She couldn't forgive me for using my fists against her father and brother, so she wants me to apologise to her parents first and then ask for her hand. It's only that damned family of hers that prevents her accepting me.

– You're fantasising, my friend. They'll never give their blessing, you know that yourself.

— But the whole village knows what I am prepared to go through for her sake. No-one can part us or deprive us of our happiness. You're a coward and an idiot if you think I'm giving up so easily.

Ruslan's last words cut me to the quick. I leapt to my feet and stared him in the face. But that wasn't enough. I grabbed his throat, he caught me around the chest and, thrusting his leg around mine, pushed me backwards. We had often practised that move in our fights at home. He fell on top of me but didn't hit me, he simply held me down and wouldn't let go.

The noise alerted Ruslan's relatives. They came in and separated us, but at least I had made clear my opinion of the stupidity of sending Zeynab back.

— If the worse comes to the worst, we'll run away again, - he repeated, as though bewitched.

— It's pathological, - I said to myself.

CHAPTER EIGHT

Mountain Goats

The next morning I was again awoken by Ruslan. He was just as agitated as before. He whispered something I couldn't catch. He seemed to think someone was knocking at the door. I slept near the door and I should have been able to hear any knocking, but there was no sound. I was about to send Ruslan to hell when a strange noise reached our ears, but it came not from behind the door but from somewhere in the distance. Carefully I opened the door a crack, and there before my eyes was a scene that you don't see many times in your life. Two huge mountain goats were locked in mortal combat. Then they backed away and stood for a moment staring at each other. They beat the earth with their hooves and charged into the attack with incredible speed. Sparks flew from their horns when they knocked their heads together. Ruslan had mistaken the sound of these blows for knocking at the door.

Watching the scene I understood why in pre-Islamic times the mountain goat was considered to be the animal god of thunder. Neither one of the combatants would give way and after each clash they retreated to their starting positions. Ruslan said that Allah himself had sent us this stroke of good fortune and we must shoot one of the goats. I ran to fetch the gun. Then we drew closer to the place of combat; we stopped about fifty metres away. One of the goats had a large wound over its right eye. Breathing deeply, I took aim. My palms broke into a sweat, my heart beat wildly and, as usual at such moments, my back ran with perspiration. Ruslan crept around to the side urging me not to miss the mark. When the goat was ready to hurl itself into the next charge, I fired.

–   The goat is wounded! The goat is wounded! - Ruslan cried. - Finish him off!

The goat really was wounded and had lost its sense of orientation. While its opponent ran off up the hill in fear, the wounded beast headed for the river. We ran after it. At a distance of ten paces I fired again and hit its back. The goat slowly sank to its knees, but the proud and wild-natured beast went on kicking its hind legs to its last drop of strength. We cheered with joy – Hurrah! Hurrah! - but we were afraid to approach it; a single blow of its horns could have killed us.

We let the animal bleed to death. Soon its eyes began to glaze over. It was a sign that it had reached the end. I was about to ask Ruslan what to do next, when quick as a flash he ran up to the goat, grabbed it by the horns and drew his knife three times across its throat. I ran down and held the goat's huge curved horns while Ruslan cut off its head. When he had separated the head from its body I lifted it high in the air and began to shout - It's ours! it's ours! This is our doing! The last drops of the creature's blood dripped onto my face, making me look like some kind of primitive savage. And right now we certainly did look more like savages than civilised people, as we leaped and shouted over the body of the poor mountain goat. It is true we highlanders are enigmas to other people - as a wolf is an enigma among other animals.

Towards midday Emi returned. He said that the situation in the village was calming down. Breathing a little more easily, we suggested to our friend that we go fishing in the river. It was his weakness. No-one could catch trout as skillfully as Emi.

The water was icy cold. We decided to climb upwards along the bank to a place where the river was blocked by trees. Sometimes trees fell right into the river, forming natural dams with the leaves and branches creating small shoals. In these places it is easier to catch trout. Fleeing from the strong river current, the fish try to hide in these shoals among the rocks and stones.

We made a fishing rod from a straight and flexible twig, fixing a line to it and attaching worms. Leaving Emi with the rod, we went off to collect wood for a fire. After twenty minutes he announced that he had caught ten small trout. Each weighed around a quarter of a kilo. Putting our catch on a stick, we lay comfortably around the fire and waited for the fish to cook.

– Just a little more salt and this gift of gods will be ready, - said Emi. The trout skin was already clinging to the tender white flesh that had swollen from the heat. I took a stick with a fish on it and nibbled it delicately to avoid burning my tongue. Emi and Ruslan followed my example.

These were idyllic moments. The three of us amidst the beauty and tranquillity of the high Caucasian Mountains, savouring delicious river trout. It melted in the mouth, I didn't even need to chew it.

– Thanks be to you, Allah, for this fantastic day, - I said, finishing my last morsel of trout. The fire burned heartily; I felt warm and immensely happy. I decided to bathe in the cold water. First we rolled some rocks across the river, then we laid armfuls of branches on top of them. Our dam soon created a little pool in which the water came up to our waists. I plunged in while my friends went back to sit by the fire. The cold water didn't shock me as I had grown used to it while building the dam. A powerful stream of water splashed over my head and massaged my body, But it was impossible to stay in the water for too long; my hands and feet were growing numb.

– What are you lying about like girls for? Come in! - I called to my friends.

They were reluctant to desert their place of warmth for the cold water. I hadn't bathed for over a week and so I stayed in for as long as I could. Personal hygiene is a matter of great importance to me. I never bathed fewer than three times a week and always wore clean clothes. Heaven forbid that my shirt collar should be a bit grubby. I would go to my mother straight away and moan that I was a member of a respected family, my forefathers were educated and reputable people, and it was a disgrace for me, their descendant, to go about in dirty clothes. My poor mother would always listen to me patiently, and say

– Tomorrow everything will be ready, Your Highness. After these words I would happily go and put on a clean fresh shirt.

And so it was now. After a week of wearing the same clothes I was disgusted with myself. My clothes smelled of sweat, dirt and everything on which I had lain down to sleep during my enforced exile. While I was floating on my back I had not noticed Ruslan and Emi enter the water. They splashed my face, we started to fight each other and then we climbed onto the stone dam and began to tumble head first into the water. After a while, Emi decided that the dam was too low so he climbed up a nearby rock face beside the water. It was about two metres high.

—   I'm going to dive into the river, - he said proudly.

I paid no attention, thinking he was just fooling around. What idiot would dive head first from two metres into water that was only waist deep? At precisely that moment, Emi slammed into the water. "He's broken his neck!" I thought. I swam over but Ruslan reached him before me. Emi's face was covered in blood.

—   What have you done, you idiot! - I shouted at him.

He was gasping for breath. Supporting his head, I plunged into the water and carefully felt around his face, neck and chest. Everything seemed to be fine, nothing broken. Then I looked at his arms; they had deep cuts. He had probably flung them out at the last moment to protect himself, and they had borne the brunt of the blow.

—   Why did you do that? - I asked when we had brought him to the bank.

Ruslan could not contain himself, and whacked Emi on his neck.

—   This morning we shot a mountain goat, dragged it home and almost killed ourselves with the effort. If you had killed yourself today, I would not have been able to pull you out. One corpse is enough for me, - Ruslan snapped at him.

—   It will be our last swim together, - Emi replied.

- What does that mean? - I was puzzled.

- You're right, it could have been our last swim. It was just that you were lucky, - Ruslan added.

- I'm serious, in September I'm going to Turkey to a religious seminary.

I glanced at Ruslan; his face registered disbelief.

I want to go to Turkey to study religion. It has to be there, I don't want to go to an Arab country.

There was a good portion of wisdom in Emi's words. Unlike the Arab countries, Turkey was nearer to us than the lands where Islam was born. After the first Russo-Chechen war of 1834-1859, many highland people went across to Turkey and from there to other countries in the near east. Even my father always recalled Turkey with fondness in comparison with other countries in the region. What's more, Turkey was a highly developed country. Since Gorbachev reformed the Soviet economy, a lot of high quality textiles came to us from Turkey – suits and jackets, along with other consumer goods.

- All right, but why does that mean you have to deliberately break your neck?

- I don't know, something made me do it. I couldn't restrain myself. I knew it would be the last time the three of us could go swimming together.

- That is interesting logic, - I said, smiling. - You wanted to scare your friends for the last time, you really are an idiot.

On the way back to the fortress, Emi said that he was going to study in Istanbul but he didn't yet know in which seminary exactly, and that he really wanted to learn about their culture and traditions there. Emi's announcement made me sad. He was leaving us and he was always fun to be around. I could joke with

Emi more than with Ruslan. Ruslan was more conservative in this aspect. He didn't like it when we played a joke or fooled around at someone else's expense, but with Emi it is different. When we were at school I only had to say to him that some girl or other in our class was ugly, and my God-fearing friend would immediately catch my drift and ask with a smile - As ugly as Aisha, or Leila, or even worse? These words were enough to launch a string of endless comparisons. Beginning with Aisha or Leila, we went on to their closest relatives, their domestic animals and sometimes to inanimate objects. These comparisons and idiotic jokes made our discussions crazier and crazier and finally, when Ruslan's ears could bear no more of this heresy, he would erupt with anger.

– It brings shame on a Highlander to speak like this! – was his refrain.

In fact we sometimes started these discussions simply to annoy Ruslan, who took the bait like a real simpleton.

Now all these fun and games would vanish along with Emi. It was as though a part of my world which had taken so long to form, had collapsed in a heap. With these gloomy thoughts in my mind, we returned to the fortress. After having something to eat, we decided to go to bed.

– What are the walls of Istanbul like? - asked Emi, as he lay wrapped in his warm felt cloak.

– Like the great wall of China, probably.

– And what's that like? - he asked, raising himself in excitement.

– I don't know, - I answered, and fell asleep.

CHAPTER NINE

The Road Home

Well it seems as though everything will turn out all right, thank God, - I repeated to myself on the way back to the village. I wanted to go home. Down there lay everything that formed my world and would always exercise its pull over me. It would be impossible ever to wash this feeling away completely. It is something that is born and dies with you. Our little yard with the big walnut tree, the walls built of smooth river stones which I liked to stroke affectionately, the huge cherry tree amongst whose fruit-laden boughs I spent the whole month of May, my mother who would die for me at any moment, and of course my father who was the origin of everything. All this drew me passionately downwards towards my homeland.

We reached the village towards nightfall. I didn't enter my home through the main gate but leapt over the garden wall at the back of the house. I found my mother alone in the yard preparing food.

— Mother, I'm back, - I whispered.

You should have seen her face. She dropped the lid of the saucepan and before I could collect my senses she had run over and was hugging me. Her clothes smelt of smoke and I almost suffocated in her embrace. She didn't want to let me go, kissing me over and over. She began to weep.

— Don't cry, don't cry, - I tried to soothe her. - I'm home, it's all over.

She didn't listen. She was beside herself with shock.

— Abdul, Zaur has returned, - she called. My mother always shortened my father's name to Abdul. My father didn't answer. She called out again and I began to worry. Why didn't he appear? Was he angry with me? Why didn't he want to see me? I hoped he had forgiven everything and was just taking his time.

Still he didn't appear. My mother called him for the third time. Those minutes seemed like an eternity. We still could not see Abdulaziz. My mother, understanding my anxiety, went over to the house to knock on his door. She had just reached the steps when he appeared on the veranda. His expression was stern; his being exuded anger.

–   Never, ever sneak into the house via the back way, jumping over the fence. If you don't respect yourself, at least respect your parents, - he said.

I remained silent and tried not to look too proud of myself. It was the first time that I had helped a friend abduct his bride and in our parts it was considered an honourable thing to do.

–   Never, under any circumstances, enter my house by leaping over the fence, jumping from the trees or by any similar means. I forbid you to enter my house like a coward with your head down. The Almighty created gates and a man of honour and honest intentions returns to his home through the gate. Then with the same stern expression, my father turned to my mother and said in a gentler tone, - Mother, feed our ignoble son and let him go to bed.

–   Oh Allah, such a weight had been lifted from me! I grinned. My father had already gone back to his room when I, with my mother's arms still around me, went up the steps into his house. That evening my mother cooked me a feast. She swiftly prepared a chicken and laid the table with my favourite sausage and slices of dried meat.

–   Eat, eat, my dear, my darling son, - she urged.

She couldn't restrain herself and began to moan, - How thin you've grown, and how did you get so dirty? Look at your nails, why are they so long and filthy?

I couldn't restrain myself either, but that was where food was concerned. My jaws already ached from chewing the tough dried mutton, but I had been so long away from such delicacies that no pain in my jaws could stop me. As I chewed I swallowed gulps of cold water.

— I can't eat any more, - I announced after ten minutes. - My stomach is full. Mother, I want to go to my warm bed, please make it up for me.

— Your bed has been ready since the day you left. Go and lie down, - she said, stroking my hair.

Thanking my mother, I went into my room and dived straight into bed. The smell of clean sheets was heavenly. It was wonderful to feel like a normal human being again. I had thought that I'd fall asleep straight away but the fullness of my stomach kept me awake.

— Never under any circumstances enter my house like that again, I forbid it, - I recalled my father's last words. They were a clue to his nature and I realised I was beginning to understand him. I don't know why it was precisely then that I felt the need to consider his words, but I began to weigh them in my mind, to analyse them. - Never under any circumstances enter my house like that, I forbid it – that was the beginning of my understanding of my father. To be steadfast and prepared to take responsibility for all your actions, whatever these may be, and to be able to stand by your principles in the face of all difficulties - only full recognition of this would guarantee that I entered through the front door of his house like a man of honour.

By which door, front or back, Zeynab entered, and where she went after that remained a mystery for Ruslan. She was nowhere to be seen. She did not come to meet him at the arranged time. Deep down I felt that things would not turn out the way the young mind of my friend had anticipated. After Zeynab disappeared, Ruslan suffered horribly. He didn't sleep at his parent's house, he got drunk, he wandered the neighbouring villages searching for his beloved. He even kept Emi and me in the dark as to his whereabouts.

CHAPTER TEN

The Arab Guest

Our return was not the only piece of news discussed in every house in the village. Doku had come home for a visit. He had been one of the first boys to leave the village to receive an education abroad and now he had a strange and mysterious aura about him. My mother said Doku's mother was going around praising her son to the skies. - Look how clever he is, studying somewhere abroad.

It meant he would become rich and famous. Everyone believed that foreign lands ran with milk and honey.

We were invited over to see him. An Arab had also arrived with Doku. In the evening I was all ready to leave when I overheard my father complaining to my mother that he didn't want to go to the gathering. My mother insisted, saying it would look very impolite on our part not to turn up.

—   I don't want to see these foreign mullahs. In two years seven of our young
    lads have already gone to Arabia to study to be mullahs. What do we need so
    many mullahs for? During seventy years of Soviet power we didn't manage
    to produce even ten doctors, teachers or scientists. In the past two years the
    number of mullahs has surpassed the number of teachers in our school.

My father was agitated, and went on complaining to my mother about the new arrival. I listened for a couple of minutes then went downstairs and outside to meet Emi. Together we walked over to Doku's house. I had no connections with him, either personal or through family. Therefore our paths in the village rarely crossed. What's more, he was older than me by several years. But I was interested in his foreign guest.

Visitors did not often come to our village, so every new arrival was celebrated as an event. Furthermore, I had never seen a person from the countries around the Persian Gulf. That part of the world seemed as distant to me as Mars and Venus. As we approached Doku's house we saw a Niva car parked by the gate. We ran over to it and peered inside. The car was almost brand new.

— Hey Zaur, look at that, - Emi caught my attention. I followed his gaze.

— Wow! - I exclaimed.

There was an American cassette player in the car, Pioneer brand. I had heard a lot about them but never seen one. They say they never chewed up tapes and the sound was very clean. It meant that the Arab visitor really was an important person. I even felt proud that such a distinguished guest should grace our humble village.

We went into the house and greeted Doku. We asked where the young people should sit. Usually, the old men and the youths sat separately.

— Today we are all sitting together, - Doku answered.

— How do you mean, all together? I asked in surprise.

— The women will sit separately but we will all sit in one room. Al Rashid wants to meet everyone in the village. We decided to depart from our traditions a little, - he replied.

I wanted to get to know this mysterious Al Rashid a bit better. On entering the room I had another surprise. It contained a foreign TV set and video recorder. Almost every family in the village had a TV set but a combined TV and video player of foreign make was something from the realms of fantasy. We all gathered around this apparatus, prodding and twiddling various knobs and thinking up interesting explanations for the function of each one of them.

– Amazing, - I said. - You only have to put a cassette in and then watch whatever film you want. It's the equivalent of having your own private cinema.

– You don't have to wait at the ticket office to get a ticket, you can choose the movie you want and not have to worry that it will be ruined by poor quality film, - Emi added.

He was right. When they brought a new film to the village, basically an Indian movie like Samraata or Zeeta and Geeta, the viewing turned into a real battle with casualties. A ticket queue would form several hours before the showing, the line would get longer until just before the showing and then a great scuffle would break out as everyone fought to get hold of a ticket. Ruslan once broke the cashier's window and cut his hand when the tickets ran out. That wasn't the last misfortune of the evening. Because of the film's poor quality the movie was interrupted in several places, calling forth a shower of abuse at the projectionist.

The realities of our life made me look upon this video recorder as a priceless luxury among a festival of beggars. I started to believe that not only an educated mullah but a very prosperous man had returned to our midst. We were all amazed. Doku's fate seemed like that of the beggar in the fairytale who one day wakes up to find himself a king.

Guests began to fill the room. We young lads gathered together, sitting huddled up in order to leave more room for the aksakkals. But I was seized by a feeling of unease and I sensed that my friends were affected in the same way. Until that point, we had almost never sat in one group together with our elders. Among the mountain people there is an unwritten hierarchy in which a young man must not sit in the company of an older man. In Doku's home we were breaking this tradition for the first time.

My father arrived with the last few guests and by now the room was almost full. Emi and I were chatting about this and that when Al Rashid appeared. He was a man of thirty to thirty-five, of medium height with a long unkempt beard and thick lips. I was impressed by his large eyes which almost never blinked. Uttering the traditional Islamic greeting, - Assalam aleikum - and pressing his hand to his heart, he sat down in the seat of honour. An uneasy silence reigned.

— Welcome to our land, - said Emi's father in Russian.

Al Rashid thanked him in the same language. Just then food was brought into the room. It was a feast fit for a king and we began to eat heartily. Doku sat down beside his guest.

— Tell us, what was life like in those far off regions? - one of the villagers asked Doku.

— Everything went well, Allah be praised. I studied in Medina and I am thinking about serving the Almighty. I was with my friend Al Rashid for all these years and when the time came to return home, he was gracious enough to come here to stay with me for a few days.

— What did you study there? - asked my father.

— Basically, the word of God, the Quran and the Hadiths, and the fundamental principles of other religions.

— And more specifically? - asked my father with an inexplicable show of interest.

Doku paused for a minute and frowned.

— The fundamentals of religion, the word of Allah in the Quran, the origins of man and the questions of suffering and evil, war and peace, jihad, the principles of mutual financial support amongst Muslims and much else.

"Jihad, what is that?" I wondered. I more or less understood everything Doku had said, except for the word jihad which I had never come across. I turned to Emi as our main expert on religious questions. Emi answered that it was a religious war.

– And why would we fight for our religion? - I asked.

Never in my life had I heard the word jihad. War with foreigners was called qazavat[10] but these wars did not have a particularly religious character. Religion in these parts served to help people face their aggressors, but it did not play a main role. No-one had ever spoken about purely religious warfare.

– Every Muslim has a privilege, that of visiting the land of the prophet Mohammed in the place where our religion was born, and a greater privilege is to study there and become a true Muslim. - It greatly surprised us that the Arab spoke Russian.

– And so in your opinion, we not true Muslims? - my father asked.

I felt that my father had something against Al Rashid. His manner was brusque. We normally treat guests with great respect, seating them in the place of honour, offering them the tastiest dishes, but my father was in a hostile mood and I didn't know the reason why.

– You live in a country which is ruled by Christian infidels. Even if your infidels adhered to the precepts of the Quran and Hadiths of the prophet, it would not be enough, - the Arab guest replied without blinking his eyes. He stared at those around him with the intensity of a hypnotist.

– Do you think that none of the people in this room understand that they are ruled by the faithless? Do you think that they are not valorous enough to prevent this, and that this great mission is entrusted to you?

---

10 After the qazavat wars, which were those in which the Prophet Mohammed personally took part

This was too much. Abdulaziz had crossed the boundaries of hospitality. In truth, he had insulted the guest.

– It's not your fault. You lived in a totalitarian country. They repressed you, deliberately destroying you and sending you into exile into Kazakhstan.

– Yes, and besides us they deported the Ingush, the Crimean Tatars, the Kalmyks, the Karachayevs, the Meskhetian Turks, the Azerbaijanis and many other peoples, - my father replied.

– You see, these infidels deported all the Muslims, - said the Arab. Doku showed his agreement with a nod of the head. The other guests preferred to observe the contest without revealing their own opinions.

– It is strange how you take such a hostile attitude towards Christians. As far as I know, you are Saudi Arabian, aren't you?

Al Rashid nodded his assent.

– Well, several hundred miles from the holy city of Mecca, the city in which the Prophet Mohammed announced his holy mission, where the holy Kaaba lies, is an American military base. A military base of a Christian country.

Silenced reigned in the room. I hadn't known that fact. My father continued in an even tone.

– As for Stalin, he not only exiled Muslims, but Russian Germans and Jews. If he hated only Muslims, he would have exiled only Muslims, so why did he have to deport Christians and Jews? What's more, if you want to insist that Stalin particularly singled out Muslims for repression, why didn't he exile other Muslim peoples of the Caucasus, such as the Lesgians, the Avars, the Dargins and others?

Al Rashid realised that he was dealing with a man who knew his history. He had probably not expected to find such a worthy opponent in this God-forsaken village. I was more astounded than anyone. After each of Al Rashid's rejoinders I doubted that Abdulaziz would find any comeback. For the Arab spoke the truth. We had been ruled by Christians; we had been deported during the Second World War. But my father's arguments disarmed Al Rashid. Under normal circumstances the Arab's reasoning would have been accepted, but it seemed weak today. I think it was at this moment that Al Rashid resorted to his final argument.

– Stalin, more than anyone else, knew that it was the Chechens who were most capable of leading an uprising in the Caucasus. Therefore he didn't deport other Islamic peoples. What threat were they to him?

This answer put smiles on the faces of many people sitting around. Our guest had shown that he had no understanding of the Chechens, of our history, or of how we viewed ourselves today.

– You evidently have a poor knowledge of the history of these parts. Long ago, when the Russians came to make war here, uprisings against the Russians in Chechnya and the Caucasus were led by the Imam Shamil. He was an Avar by nationality. Allah forbid that you ever come among a gathering where there are both Chechens and Avars and say what you've just said. They won't forgive mistakes like that. But we can leave this subject of Russians and our past and our future. - My father paused and then got up and walked calmly to the door. On the threshold he turned to face Al Rashid for the last time.

– I doubt that you love us Chechens more than we love ourselves, or care for the purity of our religion more than we do, or wish for more good for our children. Furthermore, "Not a single country shall achieve glory by adopting another country's customs". Having spoken these words he bid us a quiet farewell and left the room. After a minute we followed him. The faces of the Arab and Doku were red as they struggled to conceal their anger.

CHAPTER ELEVEN

Independence

Have you ever felt that you are not fully aware of the significance of an event but nevertheless find yourself caught up in the general euphoria of the people around you? And it takes time for you to appreciate what others have already understood. They say a fool laughs when all around him laugh – or when he doesn't understand a thing. I stupidly laughed and celebrated when, in August 1991, they announced that Chechnya had become an independent country under the charismatic leadership of Djokar Dudayev.

Of all of us, Ruslan was the most acutely affected by the new political developments. He returned to the village after spending six months in a Grozny jail. When drunk he had run into a police patrol in Shatoi. Words were exchanged and they began to fight. My friend seized a gun from the holster of one of the policemen, but at the moment he pressed the trigger another cop hit his arm and made him drop the gun. The bullet ricocheted off a pebble and hit one of the cops in the eye. The policemen lost his eye. Thanks to a large bribe, Ruslan was freed after a short time. It was all written off as an unfortunate accident.

The concept of independence superseded even Ruslan's love for Zeynab, about whom nothing had been heard. It sufficed for someone to arrive from our nearest town with news from the capital. Ruslan dropped everything and, seizing me, we ran off to find out what was going on. The new arrival said that in Grozny, Gudermes, Shali and other large towns in Chechnya they were holding a call-up for their national guard and they were giving out weapons and uniforms to all the youth and teaching them military skills. General Dudayev had apparently declared that ten years' schooling was enough for a Chechen boy, after which he should enlist in the army. He also said that Chechnya was a country that had stood up to the Russians for three hundred years and that Russia should share a part of its nuclear arsenal with us. After this speech, Ruslan's eyes blazed. He began to pace around the room like a lunatic, beating his breast, and cursing fate that at this historic moment we should be sitting at home in some God-forsaken village at the back of beyond.

And it wasn't only Ruslan who was anxious to take part. Emi phoned from Turkey to say that our students were discussing the situation all day long and wanted to return home. Only a serious conversation with his father prevented him from accompanying them, but very many students dropped their studies and returned to the Motherland.

After a few meetings with people from our district, Ruslan decided to go to the capital. The fact that he was constantly getting into fights which had led his mother to the verge of nervous collapse, could not stop my friend. Towards the end of August, at 2 o'clock in the morning, I heard a familiar tap at my window.

–   Zaur, get ready, we're going to town, - said Ruslan, grinning broadly.

I was putting together a few things for the journey when something stopped me. Another adventure, another cause of suffering to my parents, another who knew what...? I didn't ever want to see my mother in the state she had been in after I returned from the mountain. I never again wanted my father to look at me in the way he had then.

–   Ruslan, I don't want to go. My parents will go mad if we run off again. Let's drop this adventure.

Ruslan glared at me as though I had poured a kettle of boiling water over his head. Opening his eyes wide he began to curse me.

–   What crap are you talking? How can you think like this? In ten years' time they'll write books about us, make films about us. We'll make our children proud. They'll be able to say that their parents created the history of our country from its earliest days.

I realised that Ruslan was hopelessly sick, and the malady he suffered from was ideas. But I felt that I was being infected by his malady. A couple more words and I would have gone with him. Heaving a deep sigh and mustering all my self control, I said.

– Ruslan, let's drop this idea. You're not yourself. If, heaven forbid, something serious or unexpected occurs, I don't know, war or an outbreak of the plague, then we'll all join up. But right now there's no need to cast everything to the wind.

Ruslan looked at me with disappointment in his eyes.

– The unexpected has already happened. We have gained independence and that passed us by, stuck out here in the sticks. There won't be a second event like this. I can't sit here like this while history is being made. I must go, - there was sadness in his voice as he realised he would leave without me.

Without saying goodbye, he went out into the yard. I wanted to say something but his shadow was swallowed by the depths of the garden. If I had shouted after him I would have woken my parents. Then I heard the rapid pounding of hooves. Ruslan was heading for the city, to meet his destiny.

"This is also destiny," I thought, when I ran into Doku the following morning. He got straight to the point and began trying to convince me that my father and I and all Muslims must stick together and under no circumstances go against each other. I did not want to argue the point so I just mumbled something indistinct.

– My guest left this morning, he was rather offended. I don't know what they will think of us now, - he said with undisguised reproach.

– Your guest went too far and my father reacted strongly.

I took the part of my parent but then, thinking that the conversation was dragging out too long, I decided to play the role of peacemaker. - OK, Doku, let's forget it. We're both Highlanders and the rest can go to the devil. I am already tired of these discussions - I said, and sighed heavily as a sign that I wanted to end the conversation.

-   You are aware that every Muslim must know the fundamental principles of his religion.

Tell me, do you know how many pillars of Islam there are? - he asked irrelevantly.

"Here we go again," I thought. This guy is obsessed with religion.

-   I don't know, Doku, I haven't gone into religion as deeply as you have.

-   I'm not talking about deep knowledge but about the fundamental pillars of Islam which every true Muslim must understand. Come to see me next Monday and we'll have a chat. Many of your classmates will be there. You're a bright lad and in this life you have to be prepared for everything.

The fact that he said I was clever greatly improved my mood. I knew I wasn't stupid but to hear this from someone of Doku's stature was especially pleasant. For the past few months, Doku had been considered the number one guy in the village. It began when he distributed free copies of the Quran and gave free Arabic lessons. Many people wanted to read the holy book in its original language. Then he became Imam of our mosque. On Mondays he usually invited all who were interested to his home. I said I'd come.

Ruslan returned on Saturday. I don't know how he explained to his family what he had been up to in the city, but in the evening he was already up at our place. He had brought a rucksack with him which was packed full. Just as I was about to ask him about his trip, he opened the rucksack and pulled out a beret. It was the black beret of a paratrooper with the image of a wolf on its side.

-   Give it here! - I cried, and snatched it from him before he could even put it on.

In a second I was standing before the mirror admiring myself. Yes, I was made for that beret. A tall young man was looking back at me, white skinned with regular features and hair as black as coal. My eyes blazed with joy.

— You haven't seen the uniform yet, - said Ruslan.

The sight of the paratrooper's uniform, which he pulled out next, rooted me to the spot. It was brand new camouflage in the colours of late autumn. It had a whole range of features: a belt on which you could hang various accessories, a gun holster and a white under-collar. It included a pair of thick-soled boots, But the biggest surprise came next. From the depths of his rucksack, Ruslan pulled out a TT pistol. Up to that point, I had never seen a military weapon. Slowly I stretched out my hand to touch it. The metal was as cold as death itself.

Ruslan warned me to be careful with the gun. I began to spin it and take aim at the objects around me - the mirror, my clothes-rack, Ruslan. When he got fed up with this, he snatched the gun out of my hand, saying that it was his weapon and he would answer for it with his head.

— I am now a soldier in the National Army of the Republic of Ichkeria[11], and who are you? - he asked in an ironic tone. Ruslan had no doubt remembered our last conversation, when he had tried to convince me to come to town with him.

— In five minutes I too will be a soldier in the National Army of the Republic of Ichkeria, - I stood to attention. - Before the week is out, I'll have a uniform like yours, - I spoke with conviction.

— Perhaps, but you've already missed a lot. You didn't see General Dudayev, you didn't see how a thousand people performed zikr[12] in front of the

---

11 Ichkeria – the Chechen name for independent Chechnya

12 Zikr – collective recital of verses from the Quran

Presidential palace. The roar of the crowd scared even the birds from the trees, you didn't see our aksakkals brandishing daggers more skilfully than any young man, you didn't see our army parade.

I was envious. Ruslan had seen General Dudayev himself. And our new and valiant army. He had seen a thousand people performing zikr. When twenty people in our village do this it makes a loud noise. I could only imagine the sound of a thousand in front of the Presidential palace. It must have been an unforgettable scene.

Ruslan went on to tell me that the capital of independent state is Grozny. It is the capital of an independent state. Our national flag hangs everywhere; it's green, the colour of Islam, intersected with two stripes, white and red. White represents our shining future and red the blood spilled in the name of independence. Signs everywhere were already in the Chechen language. Before, they had been in both Russian and Chechen. Ruslan said that everyone was waiting to be issued with passports of the new independent country, and for a national currency. They even promised that our cars would have different number plates from Russian vehicles.

– Do you understand what I'm talking about? Something which our forefathers could only have dreamed of, for which they fought and died, has now come to pass We have become independent. Can't you see that we don't have the right to sit here at home, when for the first time in many thousands of years in the history of our people, we have become an independent country? I must be a part of this, and you must decide for yourself what you are going to do, - he concluded meaningfully.

– I've already decided, I'll go with you, - I said. - Only I want to discuss it openly with my father. I gave him my word that if I took any momentous decisions I would tell him straight away. I don't want to appear to be a liar, - I explained.

And I certainly had to speak to my father. His words that a true Highlander does not creep into the house like a coward, hopping over the back fence, still rang in my ears. I never wanted to hear them again.

I had around ten to fifteen days before the planned trip to the city. Ruslan had his own business to attend to and had to remain in the village. I anticipated a difficult conversation with my father. "If only he doesn't convince me to stay at home," I thought. My father was good at that sort of thing. To dispel my heavy thoughts, I decided to collect Ruslan and go together to Doku's house. He had promised to show us a foreign film.

Entering the courtyard, we were assailed by a delicious scent of cooking. "They are roasting a sheep," I guessed. "Perhaps they'll offer us some," was my second thought. And I was right. There were several lads in Doku's room, one of whom was a classmate of mine, but I never had much to do with him. Doku invited us to sit down and join in the conversation. There was a pile of sweets on the table with Arab and Turkish writing on the wrappers. In this time of economic crisis the abundance of Doku's table was fantastic. It crossed my mind that it had been worth coming here just to taste all these delicacies. I hastily drove that thought away. I had come to discuss elevated spiritual matters, and here I was distracting myself with thoughts of sweets. All the while, Doku was talking about some battle in the Arabian desert, a battle I had never heard of.

– When the Prophet Mohammed, peace be upon him, - he said, repeating in Arabic – Salla-I-Lakhu-alaikhi-va-salaam, - rode at the head of his detachment to fight near the Bada Oasis, he had three hundred and thirteen Muslim warriors with him and how many infidels were there?

– How many? How many? - my classmate asked.

– There were thousands of them! But they were convinced that the Muslims were twice their number because the Almighty had ordered angels to fight on the side of the Prophet. It was the only battle in the history of the human race in which angels have taken part.

Then he closed his eyes and with an air of reverence recited some long phrases in Arabic and immediately clarified that this was the ayah[13] from the Quran in the original language, praising that battle. Opening his eyes, he continued. - When the prophet's forces asked for help in this battle, the Lord replied - You asked your Lord for help and he answered you. I shall help you by sending one thousand angels, one after the other.

I was stunned by the sound of the Quran in Arabic. I had always listened attentively when my father read the holy book in Arabic. He spoke that language quite well. It seemed to me that each word in the book was some kind of secret and not from this world at all, especially when the mullahs read the Quran at funerals, which was a requirement. The words and tone of the mullahs sent me spiralling off into the cosmos. I felt that I was somewhere far away in space looking down on the earth, the Milky Way, the constellations of Leo, Orion and Scorpio, and vast black holes. The dark expanse was terrifying; I realised that I was not even a drop in the ocean, not even a molecule. Everything was in His hands, even a tiny cockroach such as I.

My thoughts returned to the room as, for the second time, I heard the word jihad from Doku's mouth. He said it was the duty of every Muslim to fight for Islam, as the Prophet Mohammed had done and all the other 124,000 prophets who had lived on the earth.

–   He who fights for his faith will receive the protection of the Almighty, and he who falls on the field of battle will immediately be lifted to the seventh level of paradise without any kind of examination or test.

At that moment, some delicious smelling dishes were brought in and we began our meal. Our host's talk continued on the same theme, - Follow the true path of Islam and you will have all that I have, money, good food to eat every evening,

---

13 Ayah (pl. ayat) – Quranic verse

spiritual riches and after your death such a life will continue beyond the grave. You will have it all.

After this inspiring speech, Doku invited us to come the following Monday and to bring our friends. Again he repeated what he had told me when we met in the street, that if he has any self esteem every Muslim must know the fundamental principles of Islam and be prepared to answer questions of religion.

– For example, - he said, gazing over towards Ruslan and me. - There are some people in the village who don't know the five pillars of our religion and that is a disgrace. Ask these people about the unworthy Christians, their scientists and poets, and they could probably talk for hours. But for them their own faith is a black hole.

I sensed that everyone in the room was looking at us. As usual in such circumstances, Ruslan acted as though he didn't give a damn. He puffed up his chest as if to say don't touch me or you will regret it, but I felt a bit ashamed. It was hard to feel like a black sheep and so I decided to keep quiet.

CHAPTER TWELVE

A Strange Incident

A heavy mountain rain fell all day; streams coursed through the streets. It was a good opportunity to get together with friends for a chat. Some classmates and I gathered at Ruslan's house. He told us some interesting tales from Grozny. At one of the meetings, while everyone was shouting and joyfully celebrating the new democratic spirit, a hundred year old man from the back of beyond sat quietly smoking. When they asked him why he wasn't celebrating, the old man replied that Moscow would no longer send us any tobacco, and because of that he was bound to live another fifty years. Otherwise, he would only have lived another twenty.

On hearing this story one of my more excitable friends fell to the floor laughing, and that made us laugh all the more. After drinking some hot tea I made my way home in the early hours of the morning. I had planned to tiptoe silently into my room as usual, when I saw a light in my father's room. Out on the porch, Ayna was filling a glass with water from the tap. - What happened? - I asked her. She said that while my father was returning from the mosque he had slipped and fallen, injuring his shoulder. I knocked on my father's door.

— Can I come in? - I asked him.

— No, Zaur, go to sleep, it's only a scratch. I lost my footing on the wet ground, - he said in a curt tone.

At that moment my mother pushed me aside and went into his room. Through the half-open door I glimpsed a bandage soaked with blood and some messy cuts on my father's fingers.

If my father had only received a scratch, then why was there so much blood and why was my mother so upset? Inside the room, Ayna was soaking cloths and administering to my father. I guessed he was sitting down, although I could see only his fingers. There were spots of blood on the floor. It seemed a lot for a minor slip.

I wanted to find out what was going on, so I asked again if I could come in. But my mother slammed the door shut, almost trapping my fingers in the wooden frame.

– Go to bed, - I heard the commanding voice of my father. He usually only spoke like that when he was very tense.

Not wanting to push my luck, I reassured myself that nothing terrible had happened, and went to lie down. In any case, Ayna was with him and, thank God, Abdulaziz was alive and well. Even if he had fallen harder than he was letting on, he would soon be okay. With these thoughts, I went to my room and fell into a deep sleep.

The next morning I knocked on my father's door again. He didn't reply. I assumed he was sleeping and went to question my mother about what had happened yesterday, where and why he fell, and how he had injured himself. She remained silent and simply told me not to ask her any questions. It was a slight injury from which he would soon recover.

– Last night you told me he had a couple of scratches, and now you say that he has a slight injury, and what will you tell me tomorrow? - I grumbled.

My mother's reserve aroused my suspicions. Why didn't my father want to see me? Why did he fall in the street which he had walked for so many years? Why had yesterday's scratch become today's slight injury? Where had all the blood come from? I couldn't figure anything out. My latest and wildest thought was that someone had attacked him. But who? And why? In our parts no-one attacked older people, neither during war nor in peacetime. It was considered an act far worse than cowardice. Perhaps they attacked him to rob him? But what did he have that was worth stealing?

Not getting any answers out of my mother, I went outside and down the road that my father had taken the day before on his way home. I had walked this path a thousand times. Every tiny detail on this narrow stretch of ground was familiar to me. The stone walls as high as a man, the neighbours' metal gates, in their gardens the half-glimpsed trees that I had climbed to pick fruit ever since I was a child. Everything was just as it normally was; there was nothing here that could have tripped my father to make him fall.

My young sensibilities told me that this story was a murky business. Something was not right here. Looking around me, I decided to retrace his entire journey from the mosque to our house. I was on the lookout for a wall that might have spots of blood on it, but even so, what would it tell me?

– Did you lose something yesterday? - asked Ruslan, clasping his head that was aching from a hangover. He had not moderated his drinking.

– No, I'm just taking a walk, - I replied.

I didn't want to say anything until I had found out what had really happened, and I didn't know anything yet. All my suspicions and guesses were based on intuition - when you are only eighteen years old fantastic thoughts enter your mind. Perhaps I was simply overly suspicious in thinking that someone wanted to hurt us.

– I'm off in a couple of days. Did you speak to your father? - he asked.

– Not yet. He's been a bit ill since yesterday. I'll wait a couple of days till he's better.

– Nothing serious, I hope?

– No, it's nothing. See you tonight outside my house and we'll talk. Perhaps he'll be better by then and I'll be able to speak to him.

– Inshallah, - he said. But my conscience bugged me.

CHAPTER THIRTEEN

The Bone Setter

When I got home I decided to speak to my father. He was already up and having breakfast on the veranda. By the look of him I would not have guessed that he had had a fall, were it not for his bandaged arm which my mother had put into a sling. Anticipating my question, he said that he was all right now, except that his arm hurt a bit.

—   I probably dislocated it, - he said, as though the matter was closed.

—   Let's call the bone setter, she'll quickly put your arm back into place, - said my mother.

—   Oh, why do we have to have a bone setter? Are we living in the middle ages? - I started to protest. I hated these village quacks who swore that they could cure everything from a cold to a hernia.

While I was moaning, my mother began to sing the praises of some woman who lived nearby and who had apparently attended all our neighbours. She said that this woman had helped a little boy who had broken his arm falling over a precipice, and another woman who had dislocated a joint carrying a heavy weight. My mother spoke for so long and so eloquently that she convinced us that this paragon used her hands as skillfully as a surgeon wielded a scalpel, and no one ever felt a thing. Anxious to relieve himself from the pleas of my mother, my father reluctantly agreed to invite the woman to come to see him. My mother made a hasty phone call and told us that the woman would be with us tomorrow.

The youthful ardour that was always getting me into trouble seized me at that moment. In a flash I was out of the house and heading to Ruslan's. I asked him to lend me the toy rubber snake he had once bought as a souvenir, I told him

I'd return it tomorrow. The snake had caught my eye from the beginning. it was very lifelike, the same colour as a live snake and formed of a light and flexible material. You could tell it was foreign-made.

The next morning a woman appeared in our courtyard, or at least a pitiful likeness of a woman. She looked utterly nondescript, a hundred kilogram lump with a face on which there was not the slightest sign of intellect. Her huge arms could probably lift a car and her eyes were like those of our cow, indifferent to everything in the world. But my mother welcomed her warmly and took her to my father's room, shutting the door in my face as usual. Oddly enough, Ayna then came back out, leaving my father with that freak show exhibit.

— Father would not let me stay in the room. He told me to untie the sling and go out, - said my mother sadly.

No sound came from my father's room, as though there were not a soul within. But twenty minutes later the door opened and the bone setter emerged. She gave me a scornful look and said that everything was taken care of. I went to the door but once again my mother shut it in my face. I asked this woman with cow's eyes if everything would be OK.

— His shoulder is badly dislocated. I don't know how he injured it so badly, but I have put it back in place.

She simpered, as though to say I'm not such a hopeless and helpless old maid, I can at least do something in this life. Her smile was a red rag to a bull. Emerging from my father's room, my mother went to her own and brought out a small newspaper packet. There was money inside. Thanking us, the bone setter turned towards our gate. I said I would show her out.

The poor bone setter probably thought I had taken a fancy to her. But in an instant I had the rubber snake in my hand, coiling and writhing. In order to make it more realistic I began to hiss. For an instant she didn't realise what was going on. Either she hadn't seen the snake or she mistook it for something else. At last she understood. She roared in an inhuman voice and ran off at a speed that any horse would envy.

I chased after her and began to poke at her with the toy snake. She ran, shouting and beating it off simultaneously. Her cries could be heard at the other end of the street as she begged me to take the snake away. She must have been mortally afraid of creepy crawlies.

– Don't be scared, it's rubber and doesn't bite. Look, touch it, - I laughed and thrust it at her again. Some kids in our street were looking at us over their wall in amazement. They also thought I had a real live snake in my hands. Soon the bone setter grew tired. Breathing heavily and weeping, she was unable to drag her hundred kilogram weight any further. She sank to the ground in the middle of the street, beads of sweat rolling down her face and shoulders. I was also tired and made an effort to convince her that the snake was artificial, but she would not believe me.

– Here, touch it. You'll see it's only rubber. It's cold, look, - I said to her. But she yelled and begged me to take it away. I kept trying to persuade her but her village mentality couldn't conceive that anyone could produce a toy that bore such a close resemblance to a real snake.

– I beg you in the name of Allah and the 124,000 prophets, take it away, - she gasped.

Every time I waved the snake at her in order to convince her that it was only rubber she wailed and covered her face with her hands. It was no use.

Nothing remained of that smug fool who had come to our house an hour ago. I was genuinely sorry for her now and inwardly began to feel guilty for starting all this nonsense. I threw the snake down and tried to lift the bone setter to her feet. The effort was enough to give me a hernia. I shouted at the idlers on the wall who were watching us to go and fetch some water. A neighbour lad brought a glassful and she drank it down.

— Fetch some more, you will probably need to go back twice, - I said to the boy. Grinning, he went off into his yard.

Having drunk two more glasses of water and not seeing anything dangerous in my hand, the bone setter began to recover. I withdrew and sat in the shade of a fence. I too was in need of a rest. After a couple of minutes the bone setter, without my help and supporting herself on her huge paws, heaved herself up. By this time all the dirt of the road was sticking to her carcass. She continued on her way, casting glances over her shoulder as she walked, as though doubting my intentions.

A minute later she disappeared around the corner. In another second her shadow vanished too.

At the time, this incident held no particular significance for me. Today's game was just one of many that I was accustomed to playing, and which I was prepared to continue playing. I could not know then that my carefree youth would end with that day's tomfoolery. Never again would I be the simple, merry lad, so full of joie de vivre, who threw himself into dances in the square with Emi. I would never again climb up into the cherry tree on the first day of spring, and sit there till evening, gazing at my village. I would never again jump lightly onto a horse and abduct my friend's girlfriend. At that moment I was leaving behind that gay and carefree life and it would never return. I could not know that then; I would not have wanted to know.

Meanwhile, the Angel Kitab, who sits on the left shoulder of every Muslim, took his book in which he makes a note of bad deeds, and wrote something down.

CHAPTER FOURTEEN

Departure

At home I found my father sitting on his bed clutching his right arm. It was clear that the ministrations of the bone setter had left him in pain. I asked him how he was feeling.

— That fool put me through hell. I don't know how I bore it. – he rasped.

I wanted to ask him if his arm hurt, but as he gripped it more tightly the question would have been out of place.

The pain in his arm did not subside during the course of the next few days. It was clear that the bone setter had made his condition worse. My mother walked around as though on needles. No doubt she knew that if it had not been for her pleas then my father's arm would not have been in that state. My father knew it too, but he never reproached her. If anything, the opposite; he knew that she had only insisted on the bone setter through a desire to help him. My poor mother, she would have gone through anything for our sakes.

A couple of days later I went to see Ruslan. The day before he had told me that Emi had phoned and would call again this evening. I had to be at his house if I wanted to talk to him. The phone rang around eight, it was Emi's voice. I could sense his smile at the other end of the receiver and picture the sparkle in his eyes.

— How are you eagles? - he asked.

— Great, but this eagle is lonely, - I answered.

We Highlanders often refer to ourselves as eagles to emphasise our proud natures.

—   Are there mountains there in Istanbul? - I went on.

—   No, but that doesn't mean I feel like an alien here. Istanbul is a diamond cast by God onto the earth. God willing, you'll see it for yourself. Its fortified walls are as high as our tallest tree. They are as broad as twenty men standing side by side.

Then he told me that some homeless people even lived inside the city walls, which were cool in summer and warm in winter. By now I was totally immersed in the conversation but Ruslan began to shout down the receiver that Emi would be bankrupted and I was making a poor student waste his money on empty chatter.

—   Come home soon, Emi, there's no-one to dance with, - I said, and hung up.

—   Zaur, you're a real chatterbox, you only think of mucking about, dances and teasing the intellectually backward. The whole village is gossiping about what you did to that poor bone setter.

—   Don't start. You and I have got up to enough things to last us for the rest of our lives. I've lost count of the number of times you've made trouble yourself, - I retorted.

—   Yes, and when was that? When we were children. And now our childhood is past. Or do you want to be remembered as a regular village hooligan?

Then he put on the old record again, beginning to talk about our country's historic mission and the responsibility of every one of us towards our ancestors and future generations. He was a gifted orator, speaking so persuasively that he managed to convince me. At the end of his speech Ruslan asked whether I was ready to come with him on his next trip to the city.

– I'm going there now but I'll come back soon. – he said. - The local district militia pestered me and said that, as a former criminal, I had to register every month at my place of residence. They were looking for a sweetener but I wouldn't give them a kopek. And you get ready, - he said meaningfully. He probably already knew about my father's problem with his arm.

– I promise to go with you and I never break my word, - I said to him firmly. I didn't like the implication behind his words. I loved my country no less than he did, but I simply lacked his inner fire, that was the only difference between us.

I asked him to send me his address in Grozny as soon as he could, so I could contact him if my father needed any medicines, and I would come to see him in the city. That way I could stay with him and not have to take shelter wherever I could find it. And so we said goodbye to each other. I returned home towards nightfall. My father was in his room, sitting in the same position as before. I thought that he was reading as usual, but in fact he was sitting with his back to the wall, staring into empty space.

CHAPTER FIFTEEN

My father's arm

Summer turned to autumn, the days flew by, probably because I now had a lot of work to do around the house. Unofficially, I had become the head of the household. I looked after the cattle, the yard, and collected stores of food and wood for the winter. For two weeks I went up into the mountains every day to chop wood and drag it home. After those two weeks my back ached and my skin was peeling with blisters from the axe. The work was gruelling, but after filling up the stores. I relaxed a bit. This winter, when all the roads and mountain paths were covered by snow and ice metres deep, we would not die of cold and hunger.

With each passing day my father found it harder to cope with his injury. The main problem was that we lived in the depths of the countryside without any medical facilities, and even when we found a doctor, they told us any old rubbish. One said salts had collected beneath the shoulder blade, others said it was not salt but infected matter that was accumulating in his body. The doctors came completely unprepared, without the necessary equipment. They only had medicine chests with bandages and iodine, and something dangling from their necks. After each visit, the doctor would come out and tell us to take my father to the central hospital in Grozny. But Abdulaziz refused, insisting that the trouble would soon pass; it was just the usual complications following a dislocation.

And so we saw in the New Year, 1992, quietly and without any celebrations. My mother cooked a delicious stew from dried meat. I normally relished our family's traditional new year dish but this year everything was different. We sat quietly together, trying not to make too much noise so as not to disturb my father. After a short while, my exhausted mother fell asleep, dropping off right at the table in front of me. I cleared the plates and went to bed. There was no more I could do. I couldn't celebrate at home and none of my friends were left in the village.

A couple of months later, Abdulaziz developed a fever. Strangely, this revived him. Regardless of his raised temperature, every morning he asked my mother to help him dress and take him down to the street. I supported him under the arm. It was still winter, and the roads were covered with snow and ice. At first he refused my assistance, but after a couple of dangerous moments he changed his mind. His arm was useless; if he had lost his balance he would not have been able to break his fall. So he began to walk to the neighbours, to the mosque and to local weddings and funerals. The neighbours also began to visit us more often. The company helped him to forget the pain for a while, even though it did not let up for a minute.

One March day, around nine in the morning, I was awakened by a cry from my mother, calling me. Leaping out of bed, I rushed into my father's room. Biting his lip and groaning, Abdulaziz's face was red with pain. His arm was twisted backwards My mother wanted to remove the sling and wrap a new bandage around the injured arm. But when she pulled the sling down, my father's arm twisted behind his back. My mother tried to tear the sling with her teeth, but the material was very tough.

— I'll get the scissors, - she called, and ran from the room.

In a second I had cut the sling. When his arm was freed, my father clutched at it with the other hand, writhing in pain. It was only then that I saw something large and swollen under his armpit. What could it be? A complication resulting from the dislocation? The reason for his high temperature? Or both? When Abdulaziz recovered and saw me staring at the swelling, he brusquely ordered me out of the room. Instead, I turned away to look at the bookshelf so as not to watch my mother helping him put on his shirt. Abdulaziz kept his favourite books on the shelf. They were mainly books by writers and thinkers of the early middle ages, such as Ferdowsi, Musa Khorezmi, Omar Khayyam, Abu Abdullah

Rudaki, Abu Raikhan, Biruni, Rashid-ad-Din, Fazlullah, Alisher Navoi and many others. My father also had books by European writers and philosophers, among them Stendhal and Voltaire. I knew how much he valued all these publications. Over the course of years he had bought the books via subscription, from private sellers and by searching them out when he was on his travels.

At my eye level was a thick book with an old cover called 'Iskandername' – the Book of Alexander.[14] I didn't recognise the author. It was a simple name of one word - Nizami. While my mother dressed my father I stood staring dumbly at the book.

I had heard a lot about Alexander the Great. He was one of my idols, as he was for many lads of my age the world over. I remember seeing his picture in a history book. On a wall in Pompeii in ancient Rome the Macedonian was shown defeating the Persian king, Darius. His large eyes, curly hair, resolute features and metal armour impressed themselves on my young memory.

When my father said I could turn round, my hand almost automatically reached out for the book and took it from the shelf. Abdulaziz had already recovered, although faint red marks still showed on his face.

—   How are you feeling, father? - I asked.

He briefly answered that he was fine. I should have said something to cheer him up, something diverting, but instead I asked him about the swelling beneath his armpit. He looked at me and then at the book that I held in my hand.

—   I wanted you to read that book when you were thirty years old. I borrowed it and read it when I was that age. But if you like, you may read it now, - he said.

---

14 Zaur is referring to Alexander the Great, also known in the eastern world as Alexander the Macedonian

It was obvious that he did not want to discuss his health. He was looking for a subject other than his illness. He never confided in me, only my mother. I didn't know why we had this relationship. I wanted to help him as much as I could, only I didn't know how.

— Very well, father, I'll read it and return it to you.

— I don't think you'll be able to do that, - he said suddenly, throwing me a penetrating look.

— What do you mean? - I asked in surprise.

My thoughts were muddled. He had spoken strangely. Seeing the surprise on my face, Abdulaziz added.

— After I read that book, I never gave it back. It's an extraordinary book. Then he looked at me in such a way that I understood I had to leave the room. As I left I heard my mother telling my father to lie down and sleep. I didn't know then that he had hardly slept for a week, and that all the while my mother had sat up by his bedside.

CHAPTER SIXTEEN

Nizami

A very long time ago, three hundred years before Columbus discovered America, a poet lived on the land that is today Azerbaijan. He was famed throughout the East and his name was Nizami. Or rather his name was Ilyas and his pseudonym was Nizami, which means someone who arranges words. Because he lived his entire life in the ancient city of Ganja in western Azerbaijan he went down in history as Nizami Ganjavi. It was Nizami who wrote the book about Alexander the Great that I had found in my father's room.

Nizami was a poet of the stature of Shakespeare and was as well known in the mediaeval eastern world as Shakespeare was in the Christian world. He was called the King of Poets at the time when poetry in the eastern world had reached its zenith. That stage of development would not be repeated in the next eight hundred years. At that time, when there was no post or rapid means of transport, Nizami's poems were read in Bukhara, in Baghdad, in Herat, and the whole expanse of land from the Middle East to the Indian subcontinent. What was it that made him famous in every capital of the ancient world? Some say it was the fact that he gave exhaustive answers to the most important questions of human existence. Such as: what is love? What is love for one's parents, for one's motherland? And what is the essential meaning of life?

Living during the flowering of the Islamic world, Nizami left not only the rich heritage of his works but also a whole range of discoveries that the Christian world only came upon four hundred years later. He described the rings of Saturn, for example, many years before Galileo Galilei did so in Italy. Likewise, he affirmed that the world was round. He also developed cures for many illnesses, and these are still in use today.

It is said that he was a man of the highest moral qualities who lived an exemplary life. In those days literary giants were often granted privileges, such as being allowed to live in palaces. Nizami refused to give in to temptation, and he maintained his independence in a world where servility was considered the norm. Because of this he was able to write about themes that others were afraid to touch.

The poem about the Persian king, Khosrov and the Turkish princess Shirin is far more passionate than any Hollywood romance. The reader's imagination can barely keep pace with Nizami's fantasy. At the end of the story Khosrov is mortally wounded. While he fights for his life for three days, Shirin cares for him, never leaving his bedside until she falls asleep on the morning of the third day. Khosrov senses that he is dying. He wants to waken the exhausted Shirin to say goodbye. But she hasn't closed her eyes for the past three days while she was tending him. Not wanting to deprive her of rest and sleep, he quietly passes away. It was his last chance to say goodbye, to speak the most important words of his life, but he valued Shirin's peace more highly than any words of farewell.

And what about the story of the love between the Arab, Majnun and the beautiful Leyli? Nizami described a scene where Majnun is living in the desert surrounded by lions, going out of his mind with love for Leyli. Majnun was in such a state that the wild animals understood that he was out of his mind with love. Even the king of the beasts decided to leave him alone,

The last of Nizami's many works was a history of Alexander the Great. Many historians have discussed the question of whether Nizami's final work was finished or not. Some said he completed it a year before his death, others say it is unfinished. In any case, 'Iskandername' or 'The Book of Alexander,' is a mythical history of Alexander that has never been surpassed, neither before nor since.

In this book Alexander goes to the Land of Darkness in order to drink the water of eternal life. Then he captures a castle with the help of magicians, he fights with African warriors and the wild tribes of Russia, and he defeats the Persian king Darius in the town of Mosul in Iraq. In a strange way all these tales would be linked to my future fate, sometimes inspiring me, sometimes offering words of advice and sometimes protecting me from making mistakes. But the most important thing is that, through the story of Alexander, Nizami would help me not only to find myself but also to understand the essence of my father Abdulaziz. Before us lay a journey where I would have to fight for all that was good - and in this fight Nizami was there to direct me.

CHAPTER SEVENTEEN

Worse and worse

While I plunged into the world of Nizami and his heroes, life for both my family and for the country went from bad to worse. Little independent Chechnya seemed poised to fight against everyone all at once: with the political opposition, which was accused of ties with Moscow; with Moscow itself; with the West; and with everyone else who was in apparent disagreement with it.

If earlier, President Dudayev had said that after independence every Chechen would become as rich as a Saudi, it was only because we had reserves of oil. Now his tone changed. He began to say all men from fifteen to fifty-five should bear arms, and in order to bear arms it was sufficient to complete nine years of schooling. He also spoke of a thousand suicide bombers who would be enough to cause a nuclear catastrophe in Russia.

My father's health was deteriorating. After long discussions with my mother and me, Abdulaziz decided to go to Grozny for treatment. We sold the cow and I used the money to pay for a private car to drive us to the city. I called Ruslan and explained our plans. Regardless of the political situation, my father wanted to go for several weeks. Ruslan warned that the situation in the city was tense; they were expecting an attack by the armed opposition. There was also the matter of finding a good doctor. Most of the best ones were Jews or Russians, many of whom had left the troubled republic.

- Give me a couple of days to look into it and I'll call you, - he said.

Then we learned that some former supporters of Dudayev such as Ruslan Labazanov, Umar Afturkhanov and Beslan Gantamirov, together with the former First Communist Secretary of the republic, Doku Zavgayev, were on the verge of leading an uprising against the legally elected government. General

Dudayev had sent government forces to fight the opposition in the west of the country. The first blood was shed there. Approximate figures gave twenty deaths on both sides. Several prominent officials, including the country's public prosecutor Usman Imaev, were taken prisoner by the opposition. Chechnya was plunging into a state of civil war.

Two days later I phoned Ruslan and he said that under no circumstances should we try to enter Grozny from the side where fighting was taking place, which he described in detail. In principle, government forces were fighting the opposition in an area several dozen kilometres from the central Shatoi-Grozny district, and therefore not directly on our road into the city. Ruslan also said that he had found a good doctor who would help my father get well. These words were balm to my heart. I joyfully ran to give my father this good news. We decided we would set off early the following morning.

My mother took a long time dressing my father, and as usual he tried to beat her off.

– Abdulaziz, wear your hat, don't forget your scarf, - she lectured him.

My father did not like to dress too warmly, even when it was cold outside. When we reminded him of this, he simply said - I lived in Siberia for twenty years, - alluding to the freezing cold there. To which my mother always answered that that was when he was young, and a few years had passed since then.

I never interfered in their quarrels. According to our customs, I had no right to do so. But I also loved to watch these scenes. In our reserved and conservative Highland society, it is not customary to show our feelings. A couple might love each other devotedly, but they keep their feelings hidden from outside eyes. The ritual of getting Abdulaziz dressed was one of the few moments when my parents displayed their tender feelings towards one another.

— Father, wrap yourself up more warmly. We have a long journey ahead of us and you have a temperature. It's no joking matter.

Having realised that he couldn't win, my father put on all the garments we had brought him, while maintaining a gloomy face. When the car pulled up at our gate I picked up our bags and put them in the boot. My mother, standing with a glass of cold water in her hand, began to cry. We kissed hastily and sat in the car. As we drove off, I turned round and saw my mother wiping her eyes and sprinkling water on the ground. It was an old custom symbolising a wish that the way would be as clear as our mountain water.

We drove to Grozny with heavy hearts, not knowing how and when this would all end. Alexander had felt the same too, when he set off on his journey to the land of darkness in search of the water of eternal life that would make him immortal. "Yes, I'd give half my life to have that water now for my father," I thought to myself, as I began to read the first chapter of the book.

CHAPTER EIGHTEEN

Alexander in the Land of Darkness

After a turbulent night Alexander awoke in a more cheerful mood. Seating himself on his throne, he called his wise men before him. "Tell me tales of marvels!" he announced. One man began to speak of the glorious city of Isfahan in Iran and its gold, the second spoke about the riches of Rey, the third praised the silk of Khorezm. There was a certain old man in this gathering who, when his turn came, spoke about a Land of Darkness, through which the River of Life flows. The old man's words caught Alexander's attention

"If yearning for joy fills your heart like a lover

Then the source of life you must discover."

—   He advised his leader.

"Are you telling me fairy tales or is there meaning in your words?" - asked Alexander.

The old man insisted that to the north there lay a Kingdom of Eternal Darkness. It was about one-tenth as far again as they had already travelled. Through it there flowed a river which bestowed immortality and absolute power. After a moment's thought the commander gave his troops their marching orders. They set off due north. After every hundred leagues astronomers performed calculations to ascertain the correct course. Thirst for immortality and power drove Alexander onwards, but his army slowed him down. Seeing that he would not get far with the entire contingent he halted on the banks of the river Volga where Turkic-speaking tribes called Bulgars lived. Alexander decided to leave the main part of his army behind with the bulk of their supplies. He would go on with his strongest and most loyal troops.

Heading further north, they began to enter a world of darkness. The great ball of the sun shrank, as did the plants of the earth. Soon they entered a lifeless expanse. If they went much further his troops would not even be able to see the man in front of them as they marched. The Macedonian soldiers had been through many battles with their commander, knowing that he would lead them to victory. But now they found themselves in unknown territory, with no idea of what lay ahead. Most importantly, how would they find a way back? Sensing his men's unease, Alexander ordered his nobles to gather together. The main question, he said - to which no one yet knows the answer - is how to find the way back after we have reached the River of Life?

The long debate that followed proved inconclusive. None of the nobility could give clear or practical advice. Then Alexander turned to his troops, and one man said he knew how to solve the dilemma.

- My father always spoke of the mare's love for its foal – the soldier began – order a mare to be brought who is just about to foal. As soon as it gives birth, kill the foal in front of its mother. When you need to return, let the mare lead the way. No matter how fierce the winds blow, or how hard the rains pour, maternal instinct will smell the foal's blood and she will find her way back to it.

Having slaughtered the foal, the troops set off. So that the army would be guided, Alexander gave his horse to his close friend Khizir. He also gave him a ruby which glowed in the night. Like a beacon for ships at sea, Khizir travelled some distance ahead, holding up the gem so that the soldiers could see him. As he set off, the Macedonian promised him:

"Having drunk the water, the road you will show me, And in accordance with God's will I shall praise thee."

Khizir rode for 40 days without stopping. He and his ruby grew fainter and fainter to his companions-in-arms. Finally he reached the River of Life. The water was as clear as a diamond and as cold as the space between the stars. It flowed softly; its babble was the sweetest music to his ears. Yet Khizir could not be sure that it was the true River of Life. To test it, he threw in a dried fish. The fish instantly came to life and swam off. Khizir drank the water, and unparalleled strength filled his muscles, making him strongest man in the world. After giving Alexander's horse a drink it began to gallop at the speed of light.

Sad to say, that having attained immortality, Khızır played a cunning trick. He decided not to return to his master. As he travelled further eastwards, the promise of immortality made him consider his destiny. No, he would not become evil and harm other people, he would not invade their lands and steal their goods. On the contrary, he would become a glorious warrior. He had seen much injustice in the course of his life. Now, and for centuries henceforth, he would become the defender of the weak. Merchants would tell their descendants the story of the mythical hero with unparalleled strength and courage, whose horse sped like lightning to aid all those in trouble along the Great Silk Road.

As for Alexander, he never found the River of Life. After wandering through the Land of Darkness for many days, he was able to find his way back with the help of the mare. On his way he met an angel who gave him a small round pebble. He asked Alexander to find an exact same stone between the high mountains ahead.

"If you find this single stone

For mortal sins you will atone"

— these were the angel's parting words to Alexander.

Alexander sought the pebble for many months. Not finding it, he ordered his men to collect stones of similar weight. Then he put a stone on one side of the scale and the angel's pebble on the other. But the pebble was always heavier. They added more and more stones and in the end they brought entire rocks, but nothing outweighed the angel's pebble.

"How can it be so? Why does such a small stone weigh more than a whole mountain! " - his men asked, unable to believe their eyes.

After thinking for a while, the Macedonian gave orders to bring dust. He put several handfuls in a bowl. It balanced the weight of the stone. And then Alexander said that life is merely dust and all that was once called Iskander[15] would turn to dust and ashes.

"Death is approaching. That was the angel's message", - he said to his friends with sadness...

Alexander's words scared me and I abruptly closed the book. My father was sleeping on the front seat of the car. I touched his hand; it was warm. "He's alive," - I said to myself, and instantly felt better. Turning my head, I looked out of the car window. To my right a side road led off into darkness.

— This is the road to Old Atagi, we will soon be in Grozny - the driver said.

After Old Atagi we drove through Chechen-Aul, Hekalo, and then reached the outskirts of Grozny. The city seemed bleak and lifeless, its drab colours resembling the Land of Darkness ...

---

15 Iskander is the Persian name for Alexander the Great

CHAPTER NINETEEN

State of Emergency

The road soon began to ascend. On our left we passed dachas, which soon gave way to five storey blocks of flats. The city seemed utterly lifeless. If it hadn't been for lights in the windows and large bonfires around which men stood warming themselves, I would have thought we were in the City of the Dead. A line of Zhiguli cars raced past us at top speed. Another couple of kilometres and we arrived at Minutka Square.

A group of armed men stood guard there, warming themselves around a bonfire. They studied us with great attention but did not try to stop us. Soon we were on the wide Lenin Avenue, driving through a lovely tunnel of trees. We reached the city centre and turned right. There we saw a huge building which I later discovered was the Dynamo Stadium. We pulled up a couple of kilometres further on, in front of a barrier whose paint was peeling off. Armed militia men stood beside it.

—   Who goes there? - a man barked as he tapped on our window.

Our driver answered that we were taking a sick man to the city hospital. The militia man switched on his torch and shone it in my father's face and then into mine. After so long in the dark, the light blinded me.

—   Get out of the car, - he ordered.

His manner was beginning to annoy me; spending many hours in a car can make a person irritable. I jumped out and opened the door on my father's side. Then I helped him out. Several men from the group approached with the barrels of their guns levelled at us.

– You have chosen a strange time to come to town. We are expecting a Russian invasion at any minute. There are spies and saboteurs everywhere dressed as civilians. For that reason, we have to check everyone, - said the first man.

My father replied that people fall ill both in war and peace-time. It is the will of the Almighty. Our interrogator came closer and asked for permission to look at his injury. I took a step forward to prevent him but Abdulaziz stopped me. At that instant I heard the click of a gun bolt.

– I'll show him myself, - said my father in a calm voice.

– Just don't make any sudden movements, my friend, - the head of the group muttered.

I held my breath. I never thought I would be so mortally afraid. My heart pounded like a hammer. My father slid his arms from his coat and was trying to pull the sling from his shoulder when the man said - That'll do.

– Excuse me for troubling you, but we're doing our job. For a whole year the city has been under a state of emergency. You're probably going to the central city hospital, it's just around the corner. You will recognise it straight away. It's a white five-storey building. At the end of the street there's another checkpoint. If they stop you, say that Anzor has already checked you. There shouldn't be a problem.

We hurried back into the car. The driver said that under these circumstances he had better spend the night at the hospital and return with us. So we reached the second checkpoint and told them that Anzor had let us through. It turned out that the hospital was just around the corner.

I helped my father alight and hurried inside to find the doctor on duty. I told him why we were here and gave the name of the doctor we sought. The duty doctor replied that Mohammed, as our doctor was called, would be here tomorrow morning. He showed us a ward where the three of us could sleep.

It was warm inside. The heating was working. This was the first time in my life that I had seen central heating. I even went over to touch the radiator, which was shaped like an accordion. After making sure my father was comfortable I fell into a deep sleep.

When dawn broke I got up to fetch hot water. Wandering the corridor in the half light, I asked the first person I met for directions. After filling a small bucket, I helped my father wash his face and hands. Then around 9am we went to Dr Mohammed's office. There were several patients already in the waiting room. I would have recognised them a mile off. They were country folk like us, in coarse drab coats and muddy boots.

After studying the other patients, I turned my attention to my father and noticed that regardless of his fever he was sitting in the waiting room without a hat or scarf. While I was telling him to dress himself properly, a short man in a white coat emerged from the office. Everyone stared at him.

—   Who here comes from the same village as Ruslan? - he asked.

—   We do, - I shot back.

He made a sign for us to follow him into his office.

Doctor Mohammed's office was even smaller than the waiting room. A cubbyhole with a table and a shelf with several books, that was all.

—   Ruslan called me yesterday and said you were coming, - he began. - It's a great pity that we are unable to offer you the best treatment at the moment. I spend most of my time on the phone begging the City Energy Department for a diesel-powered generator. Sometimes they cut off the power and what happens if they do that when a person is on the operating table, hooked up to life-saving equipment? Who is responsible for their death when it is not through medical error, but simply lack of power? - asked the doctor.

We listened attentively. He talked to us not as he would to a patient in need of treatment, but as though we were old friends encouraging him to get everything off his chest.

– We have no medicine, we even lack such simple equipment as syringes and bandages, not to mention aspirins. They promised to send them but that was three weeks ago. We are waiting for everything. – He concluded his speech by spreading his hands in sorrow as though he were a Stanislavsky method actor.

My father and I exchanged glances. Something else was worrying us. The doctor's room lacked even a stool to sit down on, and my father was too polite to interrupt him. The doctor went on for another ten minutes, saying that owing to the rise in nationalism all the good doctors who were not Chechens had emigrated. Meanwhile, the country lay in ruins.

– They say that if the Russians invade, electricity will be cut off altogether. Maybe then they'll bring us some kind of generator.

Realising that the doctor was going to talk for a long time, I took off my father's jacket and prepared to remove his shirt to show the urgency of the situation. Just then the doctor came back to this sinful earth again for the first time in twenty minutes, and asked what was the matter with the patient. Abdulaziz explained briefly but in detail how he had dislocated his arm and called a bone setter to help. Doctor Mohammed asked him to raise his arm and then I saw that the swelling beneath his armpit had not only grown larger, but it had also acquired a greenish hue. Palpitating the swelling with his fingers, the doctor asked my father if it was painful. Abdulaziz answered that he felt it but it wasn't very painful. The doctor reflected for a minute.

– You must stay here for a couple of days. Go to the first floor and have an x-ray taken, then give samples. They'll show you where to go.

Without any further questions, we turned to leave. As always, I let my father go before me. The doctor gently but firmly seized my arm and said - Come and see me this evening, but alone.

I gave a scarcely perceptible nod. At that moment my heart began to ache.

CHAPTER TWENTY

Awaiting Invasion

On the first floor my father had x-rays taken. A pale doctor with a thin moustache that drooped like worms on either side of his mouth asked a lot of questions about whether there were more swellings on my father's body. There were none, and Abdulaziz said so, but for some reason the doctor insisted that he take off his shirt. Then Doctor Worms, as I called him to myself, bent over to examine the lower part of his body, feeling around his knees, his thighs and so on. Straightening up again, he began to feel my father's neck. It was all very suspicious; I had the feeling that he knew more than he was letting on but I tried not to show my unease.

At the end of the examination, having given blood and urine samples, my father said he wanted to go out and look at the city. We went downstairs and outside onto the wide street in front of the hospital. Judging by the number of people around, we seemed to right in the centre of town. Groups of two or three men were dragging heavy sacks. We couldn't figure out what was in them. Some cars whizzed past at high speed, turned around somewhere and raced back down the other side of the road. The street reminded me of an anthill in which everyone was single-mindedly working, but on what? It was all a mystery to us.

My father was watching all these goings on with interest, when a UAZ car with blackened glass pulled up beside us. It was one of the cars that had been racing around.

— With all due respect, it is not safe at the moment to go out in the city without an escort, - said a familiar voice from within the car. It was Ruslan.

He came out smiling, grenades and pistol swinging from his belt. The guy hadn't changed; he never lost his optimism, no matter what the situation. We warmly embraced each other, and I said that if he had arrived a minute later he would not have found us.

– It would be no problem at all to find you in the city, - he said with a burst of laughter. – A thousand eyes are on every new arrival, our spies are at work.

We sat down in Ruslan's car and he began to explain everything that had been puzzling us. - The Russians are conducting a campaign of terror. Arming their supporters in the west of the country, they are putting pressure on our President in order to show him that Moscow still holds power. But the Russians won't be able to terrorise us for much longer, - Ruslan assured us.

– They are very weak at the moment, their country is in a state of collapse. What's more, the UN don't support an invasion of Chechnya, - he insisted.

– And is the UN helping to put a stop to the slaughter in the Balkans right now? - my father enquired.

– Believe me, Uncle Abdulaziz, the Russians won't attack Grozny, they are only bluffing. If they try it, it'll be the end of Russia. President Dudayev has organised suicide bombers who will blow up half of Moscow. And then, who's going to fight in Chechnya? A raggle-taggle army of drunken officers and eighteen-year old kids?

– As it happens, that would be the worst that could happen. A professional army won't destroy everything in its path, but drunken officers certainly will. But I hope all this will remain in the realm of speculation, - my father replied.

I didn't want Abdulaziz, with his fever, to waste his energy arguing over these matters and so I whispered to Ruslan to be quiet and not agitate my father. My friend managed to be silent for a minute, but as we entered the main square his excitement rose again.

– Now you'll see for yourselves, - he said as the car stopped.

We were in Grozny's main square; in former days Communist parades were held here. After the collapse of the Soviet Union it was re-named Independence Square. It was surrounded by grandiose buildings. The most splendid of these were the tall Presidential Palace and the Cabinet of Ministers building. I was stunned by the monumental office of our President. It was at least fifteen storeys high, made of toughened concrete, and at its peak it flew a huge green Chechen flag. It was the largest building I had ever seen in my life.

There were about a hundred people on the square, gathered around a large table on which lay piles of paper. To a man, they spoke of one theme, the anticipated invasion of Grozny. Ruslan said they were gathering signatures from civilians protesting against Russian interference in the internal affairs of an independent republic. These papers with the signatures of thousands of highland people would be sent out via Georgia and Turkey to Brussels and New York. There they would be put on public display in headquarters of the EU and the UN.

– Now you will see that the whole world supports us, - said Ruslan with assurance.

But his self confident rhetoric passed over my head because I was distracted by a sturdy white-bearded old man with a green bandana around his head. 'Allahu Akbar' was written on it. A small boy of seven or eight stood beside him in a similar bandana. On his shoulder the boy held a Kalashnikov.

– This is my land, - the old man was declaiming, - I don't know what the rest of the world is saying or what they think about our independent Chechnya, but no force can subjugate our people, not the Russians, nor the Germans, nor the British, no-one can crush the will of our people. No-one can bring us to our knees.

The old man spoke with such passion that the crowd grew excited. After each phrase they cried 'Allahu Akbar, Ichkeria forever!' The old man was a natural Pericles, tossed by the winds of history onto the sinful earth of Chechnya.

– Just let the Russians set foot on this land, - the old man with the white beard continued. - And they won't have enough stretchers to bear away the corpses of their soldiers. They won't have enough graves to hold the bodies. They are not warriors and never will be.

Ruslan and his driver began to shout - Allahu Akbar! Allahu Akbar! - and clap their hands. The small boy also repeated the words.

A shiver of excitement ran through my body. At that moment I realised the power of words - words spoken at the right time, in the right place, and in the right manner. With his brief but passionate declamation, the orator had won me over.

– Who can defeat our people? It is impossible to defeat a people such as the Chechens. From childhood we grow up with the stories of our heroes and the need to fight and die for our motherland. From childhood they teach us to fire weapons; they teach us hand to hand fighting.

– The Russians have nothing like that, and how can they defeat us on our own soil when we know every bush, every hill, every house, like the back of our hands? - another man took up the theme.

"If the Russians have any sense, they'll stay away," I thought, having fallen under the spell of the speakers. Without knowing it myself, I had come to think the same way as Ruslan.

My father looked tired and indicated to me that we should get back into the car. When we did so, I noticed that on the other side of the square a group of people were banging on the door of the Council of Ministers building. A few minutes later we passed some five storey buildings beside the President's office, and I saw the same group walking along the rooftops and setting something up there. On the wall of one of the buildings there was a sign: *Allah is above us, our enemies are beneath us, long live the Caucasus.*

–   What are these people doing on the roof, and why are those others boarding up the ground floor windows of the building?

–   It's just in case the Russians do decide to invade, - answered Ruslan's driver who was joining in our conversation with increased frequency.

–   My friend has a big mouth on him, - said Ruslan a bit nervously. He clearly didn't like his driver friend butting in. But it was too late, and I insisted that Ruslan tell me what those people were doing.

–   On General Dudayev's orders, we are putting the city's defences in place. There are three main zones that are being urgently prepared. These zones include the city centre, where we were just now. We have evacuated all the Government officials. Officers are training soldiers of the National Guard in Boronovka - that's where the former Soviet military base is.

"So that's it," I thought to myself. "It seems as though the situation is not as simple as it first seemed. The city is preparing itself for an all out attack."

–   But you said the Russians would never dare to attack, - my father observed.

–   We are sure that they won't. Until now, they have followed one principle: we'll bring troops up to the border of Chechnya and you'll do what we say. When we refused, they concentrated their forces on the border with Dagestan and near Stavropol, but they are afraid to advance further. But now something else is not to their liking. They have some new demands and they think they'll only have to cross the frontier and we'll fall to our knees before them. But they themselves are afraid to cross the border and then not start a war, - Ruslan spoke like a politician.

–   And if they invade, what will you do?

At this question, Ruslan grew heated. It seems that this question was one he had been considering closely. He said that they would go out in detachments of seven or eight men, running through familiar streets and buildings, striking blows at tanks, attacking the Russians from all sides. All the buildings around the presidential palace, all the rooftops and cellars were being prepared for the defence.

– Russian tanks could easily blow us off the rooftops, so we'll only have anti-tank guns up there. After firing, our men will run downstairs to the second floor, where they can fire at the soldiers in the tanks at close range. Fortified doors on the ground floors will prevent the enemy from hiding in the buildings. If we strike quickly and accurately, and most importantly, powerfully, they won't stand a chance.

– Do you see these slits in the basement walls? - he said, pointing at the walls around the entrances to blocks of flats. - We made these specially. We'll fire from these at the tanks' caterpillar tracks and at their petrol tanks. There are whole passageways through basements hidden behind sand bags. We'll be able to run along them so that the enemy can't hit us once they've worked out where we are firing from. In a word, the Russians don't stand a chance, Uncle Abdulaziz, - said Ruslan.

My father reflected for a minute and asked whether, after their experience in the Second World War, the Russians would venture into Grozny's narrow streets. To which Ruslan answered, - If they are stupid enough to invade us then they will probably be stupid enough to use tanks. Before they cross our frontier, we'll make sure we know what kind of equipment they have and the number of their troops down to the last soldier, - he said.

With that, our short drive around the centre of Grozny came to an end. Ruslan promised to be in touch in a few days. We had to wait a couple of days for the results of the analysis. In the evening I took my father up to the ward and then, making an excuse to go and fetch something, I dashed down to Dr Mohammed's office. There was no-one in the waiting room so I knocked at the door and asked permission to enter. And so began our painful conversation.

CHAPTER TWENTY ONE

Clarity amid Confusion

Although I was young, I already understood that Soviet-era doctors never told the truth to patients who are gravely ill. This stemmed from the so-called humanitarian tradition in medicine, and the desire to show compassion towards the patient. They only told the truth to the patient's close relatives. Like it or not, that's how their system worked. Therefore when I went in to see Dr Mohammed I already knew that he wanted to tell me something was seriously wrong with my father.

– Tell me what happened to your father - the doctor asked.

I told him everything, how I had seen my father that night with a bloody wound, how the bone-setter had come a few days later and treated his dislocated shoulder, and how it had become worse after that. He had developed a fever and the swelling had appeared under his armpit.

After a moment's thought, Mohammed asked me to repeat the saga of the bone-setter in detail. However, I didn't know the details as I had not been in the room while she treated my father.

– There was an instance, - said the doctor - when they brought in a young lad to see me, he was not yet sixteen years old. He had dislocated a shoulder while playing football. As is our custom, they had called the bone-setter to put the joint back. After he did so a swelling appeared beneath the boy's shoulder which began to fill with pus. Why am I telling you all this? - he asked me suddenly. - Your father has a swollen lymphatic gland beneath his armpit. This could be because it is filled with pus, so in any case we shall have to remove it. Otherwise his blood will be poisoned and result in inevitable death. But a swollen lymph gland may arise from another illness.

Here he paused. I stood before him as though I was staring death right in the face. What was he trying to tell me? That moment seemed endless. I wanted to shout - Get on with it! Tell me the bloody truth!

—   It could be cancer, like in the case of that young man, - said the doctor shortly.

—   "It's not bloody cancer! Shut up!" I thought to myself.

Mohammed said that my father had a constant fever and pallor which are clear signs of cancer. – That is the most likely diagnosis.

My brain stopped working. The doctor said something else but I didn't catch it. I had just heard a death sentence pronounced on my father. I realised I was about to lose him. My eyes filled with tears. I clutched at my head, running my fingers through my hair, pressing my palms to my forehead. For an instant my brain switched off from this sinful world. I don't know what I did during those moments or how long they lasted.

Finally I gathered my senses a little. - How long does he have left? – I gasped.

—   If he's lucky, a year and a half; if not, six months. It all depends on what stage the illness has reached and how fast it progresses.

I stepped towards the door and turned the handle.

—   Zaur, I have to tell you that if he has a strong heart then his death will be protracted, and then it will be a horrible death.

At these words I felt sick, for I knew that my father had a strong heart. Closing the door, I hurried to the toilet and washed my reddened eyes. I had to go up to the ward now, so I didn't want my father to see the state I was in. One look at me would be enough for Abdulaziz to understand everything.

When I reached the ward I found my father already in bed. "How could he get undressed by himself?" I wondered. I asked if he wanted anything. He asked me to put a glass of water on his bedside locker. With my head bowed so that he couldn't see my face, I did as he asked. Then I lay down fully clothed in my bed. Thrusting my head under the blanket, I burst into tears. I held the blanket with one hand and pressed the other across my mouth so that my father could not hear my sobs. When it became too hot I stuck my head out from the blanket, took a few breaths, and then covered myself again.

"What will become of him now? How long will he be with us? What shall I tell my mother? She won't be able to bear the truth." The thoughts circled my head with the speed of light. Soon my head began to ache. Then i told myself to calm down, for at any minute my father might ask for me. Now was not the time to weep like an old woman. Several hours passed while I remained in this state. At about three o'clock in morning, I had recovered enough to emerge from beneath the blanket.

I could see nothing in the darkness. After a few seconds my eyes made out some objects in the ward. I knew that Abdulaziz slept very badly at night because of the pain. In a low voice I asked if he was asleep. He replied that he was not and asked why I wasn't sleeping.

— I was asleep, I just opened my eyes for a minute and wondered if you needed anything?

— Let's hope to God they'll be able to cure me soon, the pain is getting worse. It wears me out, not allowing me to sleep normally. I'll get well, don't worry, - he answered. - Go to sleep. Tomorrow we have an important meeting with the doctor, - he added.

In the morning I got up and quickly dressed. Bringing hot water, I helped my father dress and filled the bowl with water for his morning ablutions. Then I wrapped his head in his scarf as my mother had requested. Only now did I notice how pale he was. We probably hadn't noticed before because we saw him every day, but after last night's conversation with the doctor I saw everything differently.

Half an hour later we were in Dr Mohammed's office. He reassured my father that everything was fine and the swelling was simply filled with pus. Tomorrow at 7am they would operate, and after the operation it would all be over. Abdulaziz was very happy. He started to say that he had thought it was something else and that the treatment would be long and painful.

– I thought that I only had a few years left and that I'd never see my son grow up into an educated and successful man.

– Get along with you now, my respected friend. You'll be dancing at his wedding and then playing with your grandchildren, - said Mohammed.

I took my father's arm and said - Thank God, everything will be fine. Abdulaziz was in seventh heaven. We went on talking about my studies as though they were a lot more important than his illness and tomorrow's operation. Leaving the hospital, we enquired how to get to the telegraph office. From there we phoned home. My mother was overjoyed to hear us. She was scared when we told her about the operation but I said it was nothing. Ayna promised that as soon as we returned home, she would cook my favourite sausage in sauce, which was one of her specialities.

In the same cheerful mood, my father went in for his seven a.m. operation. That day Ruslan and two of his friends, armed to the teeth, went to the Central Energy Company and told them that under no circumstances were they to switch off the power in the district where the hospital was situated. The director swore on all that was holy that he had already received instructions over the phone and he would keep the power on. That was not enough for Ruslan. He stood by the man's side for two hours while the operation was taking place, looking so menacing he scared all the workers there.

The operation itself took an hour, as planned. My father had not yet woken up when Mohammed asked me to come and see him. He said the situation was worse than he had expected. My father's cancer was in its final stages. As soon as he had opened up the injured shoulder the doctor had seen what he called metastases.

– Nothing will help him now. Go home. If it wasn't for this turmoil, it might have been possible to send him to Moscow for chemotherapy, but it would only prolong his life for a year at best.

I listened to him with bowed head. It was as though I were hearing a judge pronounce a death sentence. I came to my senses just as he finished speaking.

– Now only morphine will help. He'll need three injections a day. I'll give you a prescription saying your father has cancer and you will get three boxes of morphine from the dispensary. They contain 12 capsules each. That will help to ease his suffering.

I took the money for the operation out of my pocket. Mohammed didn't want to accept it but I insisted. While my father was still unconscious, I picked up the morphine from the dispensary and called our driver. He said that he would be in the city in two days.

As we drove away from Grozny I pretended to be in a good mood, clowning around and cracking jokes, but inwardly I could only think of Pushkin's tale, 'Feast in the Time of Plague.'

CHAPTER TWENTY TWO

Welcome to Hell

On New Year's Day 1995 our phone rang. It was Ruslan. I thought he was calling to wish us a happy New Year. I was not in a good mood and didn't want to speak to him for long, but out of politeness decided to talk for a few moments. I was in no New Year mood but what Ruslan told me made my spine tingle.

–   It's not true, you're lying! - I cried. Ruslan had told me that they wiped out a large Russian convoy in Grozny the day before. If Ruslan was to be believed, it was not just a military operation but a true rout of the Russians. He said that in the space of five hours his detachment destroyed the first column of invaders travelling along Pervomaiskii Street. A huge column of sixty tanks and other military vehicles had beene coming from the direction of the northern airport, shooting at anything that moved. Their first victim was the driver of the small Zhiguli car that was passing the Council of Ministers building and heading towards the railway station. His car was shot by the gunner in the leading tank.

–   The Russians thought they could mow down everything like in a shooting gallery. Right up to the last moment they never suspected that they were being drawn into a trap prepared by the Dudayev Division. So certain were they that we would offer no resistance, that they went into the city as though they were on a military parade. The soldiers and officers in tanks and military vehicles didn't even have correct maps of the area; they advanced in bad weather and without support from the air. When the columns reached the centre of town, the Russians did not even put soldiers along the route to provide cover from the rear if something happened.

–   And so why did they invade if they were not properly prepared and the weather conditions were so poor? - I asked Ruslan.

His reply made my blood run cold. - It seems that the 1st January was the birthday of the Defence Minister, Grachev, and his lackeys wanted to make him a present of the city of Grozny. I remembered a history lesson at school, when Aïsha Rasulovna told us that in 1945 Joseph Stalin ordered his troops to take Berlin on the 1st May. Marshal Zhukov, who was given the order, didn't fulfil it until the 9th May. Because of this whim of Stalin's, as many soldiers were killed in Berlin as the USA lost in the entire Second World War - around 200,000. It seems that the thinking of the masters of the new "democratic Russia" differ little from that of the Politburo in Stalin's time.

I then discovered that towards evening the advancing Russian forces, in the euphoria of victory, had entered the Presidential Palace and gone on air to announce the success of their New Year's Eve operation. An unknown voice simultaneously announced - Welcome to Hell! That was the signal for our forces to spring out of their hiding places and attack.

In the course of five hours about 200 Russians were killed, including some of the sub-divisional commanders who had so irresponsibly launched the operation. Ruslan said that the defenders let loose a hail of fire from the rooftops down onto the tanks. Signal rockets dropped grenades attached to small parachutes. These exploded on the heads of soldiers and officers who were fleeing from the burning tanks. In a word it was absolute hell.

When other divisions heard what was happening by the Presidential Palace, they simply refused to come to the aid of their brothers. The same happened with the divisions who were summoned the following morning. Instead, the remaining troops decided to take civilians as hostages in order to somehow save themselves. But our forces were better prepared and all civilians had been evacuated from the city centre several days before the invasion.

On hearing this news, I couldn't restrain myself. I held out my arms and threw myself into one of our highland dances. The noise brought my mother into the room and she told me to calm down. - Be quiet, Zaur, your father has only just shut his eyes, - she whispered. I was in such a state of euphoria that I had quite forgotten myself, but her anxious words pulled me to my senses.

And so began the confrontation that has gone down in history as the first Chechen war. This war cost the lives of tens of thousands of civilians. Five hundred thousand fled as refugees. The war was tough for the Russians too. Official figures state that fifteen thousand soldiers and officers were killed. But on that day I could not know this. Ahead of us, hell awaited.

CHAPTER TWENTY THREE

Alexander Defends the Caucasus from Wild Russian Tribes

It was already two weeks since Alexander had returned to his homeland, Pella, from his expedition to the Land of Darkness. He usually spent the first part of the day with Aristotle and the second in the merry company of his companions in arms. But one of them, the valiant Duval, the ruler of Abkhazia, was missing. Enquiring into the fate of his subordinate, Alexander discovered that Duval was on his way back to the Motherland with news. Two months passed and then the king of Abkhazia fell to his knees before Alexander.

–   Lord, the number of Abkhazian dead is incalculable. Countless citizens have been slaughtered. The wild Russian tribes have sacked Barda and Derbent. Thousands of women and children have been taken prisoner and our storehouses have been destroyed.

Duval said that if they did not march out to stop the enemy they would also seize Khorasan from Alexander. The great leader was moved by this impassioned speech.

–   If I can't beat these lions, I'll be worse than a dog in their eyes, - he replied.

He immediately organised his troops for the march, calling together all the remaining commanders from his empire; Koum came from Iran, Bushek from Khorasan, Duibess from Mediana, Gur Khan from Khotan, Khindi from Rey, and dozens of others. He swelled the ranks of his army with thousands of Turks who inhabited the wide expanses between the Caspian and Chinese seas. Some of his commanders tried to persuade him not to use Turks in battle.

–   The Turks may not think like us, but they too are enemies of the Rus, - Alexander replied.

The military leaders pondered on his words. Choosing the right moment, Alexander emphasised his argument by telling them a tale.

–   Do you know the story of how the fox who was being chased by two wolves managed to escape them by barking? - he asked.

The warriors looked at Alexander with curiosity, not knowing what to reply.

–   The two wolves were chasing the fox in order to tear her to pieces and eat her, - Alexander began his story. - And the fox's fate already seemed to be decided, as the wolves were almost biting her tail. As she ran past a village, she began to bark loudly and all the dogs answered her. Everyone knows that dogs hate foxes and wolves.

–   Waking up the whole village, the dogs ran in the direction of the vixen's bark. As a result, the wolves took fright and ran away in panic. That was how the fox saved her life.

–   When the road is hard, be not afraid, free yourself from your enemy with enemy aid, - Alexander concluded.

As they had already seen a hundred examples of Alexander's genius, his commanders bowed to his suggestion, and Turkish soldiers poured into the ranks. In a couple of weeks they were marching through the Kipchak steppe and then encroaching on territory that was controlled by Russian tribes. Two armies, which seemed to resemble two seas, locked in mortal combat. It was a terrible battle in which the screams and groans of wounded soldiers made horses rear up in fright, where the throat dried up with thirst, where you could not put your feet on the ground among the piles of corpses, and the archer's arrows could not even reach the earth when they fell.

Seated on a white elephant, Alexander valiantly and furiously fought at the head of his army, but long hours of battle brought no decisive victory. As the sun sank towards the horizon, the armies retreated to their camps. The next day the battle would be even fiercer.

In the early morning the Rus sent a strange creature into battle. It looked like a devil from hell, with big horns, skin as hard as stone, arms that could crush diamonds into dust, and thick legs bound in chains. It carried an iron pole with a hook at the tip with which it swept up men with one movement. The Cyclops turned its prisoners into a bloody mess. One after another dozens of Alexander's best soldiers were caught by the hook, and the monster tore off their heads and legs.

For the first time in his life Alexander was gripped by panic. What was he to do? How to defeat this creature from hell? Being a strong believer, he was convinced that the appearance of this creature was a sign from above, and it meant he was destined to die here on the mountains of Abkhazia without fulfilling his mission. But he would not have been Alexander if he had not tried to find a way out of the situation. He quickly called together his highest officials.

– The situation is impossible, - said Alexander. - We have to find out everything we can about this creature, who he is, where he comes from, what he eats, when and where he usually sleeps, and how the devil he got involved with the Russians.

The answer came fairly soon. One of Alexander's aides discovered the story of the monster and related it to him.

– In the Land of Darkness, where you sought the water of eternal life, there is a mountain. Beings live there who are similar to humans but their skin is made of iron. No-one knows where these monsters came from or how they got to this earth. No-one has seen their bodies and no-one knows which sex they are. They eat only sheep. When night falls, they thrust one of their horns into a branch of the largest tree they can find and there they sleep, hanging from the branch. They sleep deeply, and because of this, the monster was taken prisoner. Its captors bound it in metal chains and attached heavy ropes to it. All the Rus joined together to pull it down. If it could tear off its ropes and chains, then the monster would kill its captors. If not, it will remain prisoner for its entire life.

Alexander reflected. His troops were losing heart. Even the bravest among them were starting to fear going into battle. It was down to him to restore their faith in victory. Tomorrow morning he himself would do battle with the monster. Having made his decision, he asked his astrologer to look at his horoscope for the following day.

—   Let the tulips hide in the mountain crevasses, your sharp mind and sword can penetrate these peaks, - the astrologer replied.

—   That's settled then, tomorrow I'll bring him down. I even know how, - said the Macedonian.

In the morning, the two armies lined up face to face. The Rus brought the horned monster in chains. Alexander was seated on his white elephant. To his right stood the Chinese army with the best metal pots full of oil; on his left, the Turks. When their opponents sent the monster into the field, the Chinese hurled the pots and covered every millimetre of the ground around the monster with oil, which they then set alight. The monster was surrounded by flames. Alexander sent three elephants into the flames to trample the beast, but as soon as they entered the flames, the monster grabbed one of them and with a single movement, tore its trunk from its head. Pouring with blood, the animal fell dying to the ground. This scene horrified Alexander's forces and cheered the enemy. Now they scented victory.

—   Another second and all will all be lost, - the commander cried, and drove his own elephant straight into the action. His troops held their breath. A minute later Alexander's silhouette disappeared into the smoke. Another minute passed and then five, but he still could not be seen. The Rus were poised for the attack, their prince had his troops ready. The enemy camp scented imminent victory. The Russian prince held his arm aloft as a signal to attack, when amidst the dispersing gloom they beheld a scene they would remember for the rest of their lives. Alexander was seated on the monster, which had collapsed to the ground. He was beside himself with joy. Now nothing could hold him back from vanquishing the Russian hordes.

— There is a reason why Homer's Iliad is my favourite tale. I knew that the monster would have an Achilles Heel and that it was his neck. I noticed it only when I was close up. I threw my lasso around it and tied the end to my elephant's legs. The beast pulled the rope until the monster's neck broke, - he explained later to his troops. Alexander defeated the Russian tribes and liberated the Caucasus.

The story filled me with an indefinable energy. Closing the book, I understood that there are things that are pre-destined for us. Alexander was destined to conquer the Russians in Abkhazia[16] and I knew that we were destined to defeat them in Chechnya.

---

16 Abkhazia is a breakout region of Georgia today, de-facto controled by Russian forces.

CHAPTER TWENTY FOUR

General Mobilisation

On the morning of the 2nd January 1995 I awoke in another country. At eight o'clock I went to the mosque in the village's central square. Prayers were already taking place. Old people and young alike were clapping their hands and crying - La llaha illallah, - which means 'There is no God but Allah' in Arabic. I joined in. Beating out the rhythm, I began to chant - La ilaha illallah. In a second I was gripped by the general euphoria and hypnotised by the crowd. I was waking up to a feeling that is aroused in all extreme situations. After the zikr, the elders announced that there would be a holy war, a jihad against Russia.

As the chief imam of the village, Doku spoke. He said that a few minutes ago the chief imam of Chechnya, Akhmed Kadyrov, had announced on the radio that all men from 15 to 65 were called to fight a holy war. He also said the imam had called on every Chechen to kill 150 Russians. Then we would defeat Russia. They arranged for us to gather in the square at three o'clock in order to travel to our district capital. There we would be met by leaders of the resistance and they would give out arms and further instructions.

I went home. I didn't know what to do. My father needed constant care and my mother had reached the limits of her strength. She rose when he did and went to bed when he did, but my father slept only two or three hours in twenty-four. If I went to fight, who would be there to help my mother? Who would get his medicines, especially morphine? I would have to go and speak to my father. He usually slept in the morning, so I decided to wait for a couple of hours. My mother asked what they had been saying in the village square. She was obviously very worried but she maintained her dignity. After my father awoke I went in to see him.

He grew thinner by the day and his face had turned yellow. It was hard to look at him. For as long as I could remember, he had enjoyed rude health which showed in the redness of his cheeks. Now all the signs of that good health had disappeared. Without wasting time I told him everything I had seen and heard. Abdulaziz struggled to sit up and I hastened to adjust his pillow so he could lean back against it.

— So where is your brave UN, your OSCE? - he asked straight away. - Are they discussing what the Russians have done in Grozny? Are they going to give us some help, apart from empty chatter? - He sighed heavily, and continued, - It's already a question of principle for the Russians. If they don't take Grozny, they'll be shamed before the whole world, so that can't be allowed to happen. They will send in as many troops as they need in order to capture the city, and our young men will die in their thousands.

I listened attentively, but said nothing.

— Go and fight. Your mother and I will manage somehow. Only be careful, your mother has no-one except you. As he spoke these final words, a lump rose to my throat and my eyes filled with tears. I felt like death. He knew that he was critically ill. Why had I tricked myself into thinking that he didn't suspect anything? He knew it all very well.

"I'll have to leave the room right now, or else I'll burst into tears," the thought shot through my mind. For the first time in my life, I kissed my father's hand. Rising quickly, I left the room, then I went out into the back yard and sat in our big walnut tree. I could not hold back my tears.

At three in the afternoon we climbed into a Kamaz lorry and drove out of the village. A procession of mothers, sisters and brothers saw us off. Many brought food and water for the journey, although it was only a thirty minute drive. No-one cried, everyone was calm and collected. As we drove out of the village I saw a black flag hanging on the pole, together with our national green flag. This was the flag of the followers of the so-called True Islamic Faith. I could not decipher the Arabic writing on it. In peacetime Doku would not have been allowed to do this but right now people's minds were on other matters.

When we reached the capital of the Shtoum-Kale region, I realised the true scale of the tragedy. The first refugees were arriving; they came in open trucks, in cars and on motorcycles. They drove out of Grozny in anything that would take them, and in a severe frost. "How did they not freeze to death on the road?" I wondered. Our lorry stopped in the main street, which reminded me of a bazaar during rush hour. Locals were running back and forth from their houses bringing anything they could from their houses - hot tea and soup, milk for infants, warm clothes - everyone tried to do what they could.

Ten metres away, a woman of about 35 was in hysterics, and several others, also in tears, were trying to calm her down. Her face was covered in blood. At first I thought she had been wounded, but then she began to beat her face and fresh blood poured from her wounds. She tore at her face with her nails. - My children! My children! - she shrieked. In order to calm her down someone tried to hand her a glass of water, but she dashed it to the ground and began to shout and call her children again. We were frozen in horror by the sight.

— She has left two children behind in Grozny; we took her away by force. She thought the Russians wouldn't invade and so she sent her children to her sister on the other side of town. And that's where the Russians began their attack. Now she doesn't know what's happened to her family, - said a fifteen year old boy who had arrived with the group.

Like a dummy, I stood staring at the woman, unable to tear my eyes away. Her grief seemed to be mine too. Soon she broke away from the group around her and began to dance. Raising her arms in the air, she danced as though nothing had happened. But blood ran down her contorted face and neck. "She's lost her mind," I thought. I wanted to sit down somewhere.

- There are thousands of children left in Grozny, they are all hiding in basements. They say that since the morning the Russians have been bombarding the city mercilessly with artillery and from planes, - the same boy added.

- Soon the people from the militia will come, wait here for now, - someone said. And so we spent several hours amid these harrowing scenes. With each minute that passed I felt worse. In order not to see or hear anything more, I pulled the flaps of my hat over my ears and buried my head in my collar.

After witnessing this suffering many eyes burned with hatred. People wanted only to be given arms so they could go into battle themselves. Not one of us gave a thought to the fact that we were not professional soldiers and neither were our officers, and that we didn't know where and how to shoot. People were simply gripped by emotion. It was then that I understood how attached we were to this soil, how much we loved this land and our brothers and sisters who had been killed in Grozny. It was a truly patriotic war, a people's war against an army of occupation.

Around three o'clock in the afternoon I saw a familiar UAZ car heading towards us. It was the car which had stopped outside the hospital in Grozny and driven us around. Therefore when I saw Ruslan emerge I was not surprised. He was accompanied by a couple of burly men in full military uniform. They lined us up and Ruslan told us what we already knew. - A furious battle is raging in the city. After we destroyed the first Russian detachments, they held a call-up throughout the country and the best divisions were sent to Grozny. From that moment the battle in the city became more vicious.

Ruslan ordered us to come up one by one and take a Kalashnikov and two grenades from his companions. One of them held up a grenade and began to explain its features. He said the grenade was called an F1 and was ideally suited to military combat within urban areas. Before pulling the pin you had to throw it from a place of cover. It could be the corner of a house or a dugout, for example. Otherwise the grenade could injure the thrower as it exploded. They also said that later today on the outskirts of town they would train us to use the guns.

After this short course, the Kamaz pulled up and they told us to get inside. When it was my turn, Ruslan grabbed my arm and pulled me aside.

—   What are you doing here? You find time to play the hero but who's going to help your father get his medicine? - he asked.

Reluctantly I replied that I'd fight for a couple of days and then return home.

—   Are you an idiot, or what? Half of Russia will soon be fighting in Chechnya and you say you'll go home in a couple of days. There's going to be a huge battle for Grozny. I told you that it's only just begun. I'll be back in a couple of weeks and we'll need more people then. You can go and fight then, but for now go home and help your father. Right now you are needed there more than you are here.

Not giving me time to gather my wits, he got into the UAZ and shouted to me, - Go home, your father needs you now. I understood that he did this so that the others would not think badly of me. He was protecting me, although I would rather have remained by his side.

After a few hours' training those lads went off to Grozny. The next day, January 3rd, the Russians bombarded the town of Shatoi which lay in the path of our volunteers. Three hundred civilians died, among them many young children. But the volunteers reached Grozny and engaged in battle with the Russians. For two of my classmates, it would be their last battle.

CHAPTER TWENTY FIVE

Thick Cigarette Smoke

I returned to my village with mixed feelings. On one hand it was hard to sit on the sidelines while my peers were going to fight and die in Grozny. On the other hand, my father's condition had deteriorated. He was literally wasting away before our eyes. The fever never left his emaciated body, he could barely walk and his right arm had withered to the bone. He had begun to smoke heavily. I realised that soon it would be hard for him not only to shave, wash and dress but even to move. He spent most of the time in his room.

My mother did not leave my father's side for a minute. She had become his guardian angel. I don't know why, but he didn't allow me to remain for long with him in his room, especially when the pain was at its most intense. He asked me to leave him and not witness his suffering. After a while I understood why. It was not our custom to complain, wail, groan or to show our weaknesses before others. We were supposed to face all situations and problems with dignity and with our heads held high. And so perhaps he still wanted to be an example to me, so that for me too when the time came, I would not lose my dignity, no matter what the circumstances. But would I be able to live up to his example?

Whenever Abdulaziz had an attack of pain, my mother went in to him and tried to help. She gave him a morphine injection three times a day, but in less than a month my father was complaining that morphine no longer helped. At night the kerosene lamp in his room was never extinguished. Abdulaziz fell asleep only towards morning, and then just for a couple of hours. In order to let my mother sleep for a while I would prepare his breakfast in the morning, and tell him the latest news. I took care to speak in such a way as not to arouse his anxiety. One theme which I avoided entirely was the war in the Republic. He would become extremely agitated if the conversation touched on that subject.

My father's mood was generally lighter in the mornings. At this time of day Abdulaziz appeared more like the healthy and cheerful man that I had known since childhood. - I sometimes envy you very much, - he said one morning, to my surprise. - I'm almost sixty years old and I was never overwhelmed by parental love, but almost every night for twenty years I dreamed about my mother.

He related how in his dreams he would hug her and stroke her soft fair hair. And then he would get angry when his relatives woke him in the morning and sent him to work in the millet fields.

During the Second World War he and his mother had been deported to Kazakhstan, along with thousands of other Chechens. Later, after his mother had died and he found her remains he could not touch her bones for a long while. He would simply sit by her grave and gaze at what remained of that most blessed being, as she had once looked on the little Abdulaziz, the only thing left to her in the whole world.

When he re-buried his mother in their native village, she stopped coming to him. - I would love to see her again in my dreams, I'd give anything to have her tender hand smooth my brow, kiss my cheek and say she loves me just as before. I could endure anything for one of those moments, - he said.

I felt terrible. It flashed through my mind that soon I'd be prepared to give anything just to sit here in the early morning and have a heart to heart talk with my father. The wish was as ardent as it was futile. Having smoked his cigarette, Abdulaziz went on to talk about how he'd applied to law school in Sverdlovsk. Every year, in the column of the application form that asked who his parents were, he wrote 'repressed kulaks'. This meant that he would never be accepted into a prestigious institution. He handed in his documents all the same. Then he turned up drunk to the examination on the history of the Communist Party of the USSR, the most important subject in those days, and created a scandal. They asked him not to write that his father had been repressed as a kulak and to join the Communist party, but he always spurned their advice. - That was what I hated most about Communism, - he said bitterly. - That was its fundamental problem. In order to live in this country and achieve something you had to renounce your principles, your parents, your kin, your ideals. And after that what would I be? Nothing but a corrupt and well-fed animal. That's why Nizami said, - Let them steal. For me it's a relief that no-one can take me for a thief.

– You must understand that it is better to live as an honest man in our village than as a corrupt minister in Moscow.

– Does that mean they're all corrupt in Moscow?

– Not all, but the honest ones are lost in the general mass of careerists and stool pigeons. For the system rests not on honesty, courage and an upright approach to your work, but precisely the opposite. As a result, people like Gorbachev become leader of the USSR and destroy it in the space of five years. He did what even Hitler never dreamed of, - Abdulaziz replied.

I smiled. My father was right, Hitler with his 138 armed divisions could not destroy the USSR, but Gorbachev did it in five years in peace-time. Now, three years after the collapse of the Soviet Union, the Russian air force is bombing one of the country's former cities in which a quarter of a million civilians live.

CHAPTER TWENTY SIX

The Approach to Grozny

While I was sitting with my father his morphine ran out. Abdulaziz said that cigarettes helped him more than morphine and that he didn't need it any more. But I didn't agree with him. If morphine didn't help the physical pain it helped to calm his mind. My mother agreed that he rested better after an injection. But they weren't enough to help him bear the pain. We only had one box of twelve capsules left – enough for four days. I had promised Ruslan that I would return to the regional capital in two weeks but by now two months had passed.

Early in the morning of March 1st I put on my body warmer and, taking my gun and the grenades they had given us last time, I slipped out of the house and went down to the village square. There I got into the first passing car and drove to the regional capital. Like last time, it was full of refugees, but they were not running around in despair. Most of them had been accommodated in schools and administrative buildings. Local people had provided them with all the necessities, but the sad thing was that the number of refugees was growing. There were a quarter of a million people in Grozny and they were streaming out towards the south of the country, ahead of the advancing Russians. There was not enough room for the wounded in the town's single storey hospital. A crowd of young men had formed outside the hospital building. I went over and greeted them. In two minutes they filled me in with everything that was going on.

– In a minute, the instructor will come and we'll set off towards Grozny. Right now, it's like Stalingrad. A cruel battle is still raging. We're fighting for every house, every entrance-way, every staircase. The most terrible bloodbath took place at the Presidential Palace and the Council of Ministers. The buildings changed hands several times but now the city centre is in the hands of the Russians. It's absolute hell there.

The young lad who related all this introduced himself as Said. He had just arrived from Kyrgyzia where he had studied in a religious seminary. Said told us that he would be our co-ordinator in Grozny, as he had grown up there.

Very soon a man of around thirty turned up. He told us to get into a bus and we set off in the direction of Shatoi. We drove very fast in the hope of avoiding any potential bombardment. There were a lot of tents along the sides of the road. People were camping wherever they could. Trucks came past us loaded with people. Some were crying, some wildly gesticulating. In their anxiety they all looked very much the same, but then two little boys aged five or six flashed past, riding in a tractor trailer filled with rubbish. I turned my head so I could watch them for a bit longer. Amidst all this hellish confusion, amidst the tragedy that had befallen the people, those boys went on joking and fooling about with each other. One was trying to pull a bicycle pump away from the other, who hit him on his head. They looked so different from the unhappy faces around them that their childish play made me smile.

We spent less than an hour in Shatoi. From there we drove to the village of Prigorodnoye, which is right on the outskirts of Grozny. There were more people here than in Shatoi. Some had come to fight, others were searching for relatives or making their way to Grozny to find out what had happened to their apartments and belongings. Said suggested that we climb the heights between Prigorodnoye and Chechen-Aul. From there we would be able to see the suburbs of Grozny.

Five or six of us began to climb. When we reached the top of that nameless hill, we were able to see yet another convoy leaving the city. It consisted of two trucks with white flags hanging from their sides. From our viewpoint we couldn't see who was inside, military or civilians. The trucks were driving fast. Then two planes appeared and swooped down to attack the convoy, diving low and firing on them.

We watched as though hypnotised, not knowing what to do. The first bomber, flying above the trucks, fired a rocket. It missed its target and exploded nearby.

The driver of the truck in front swerved off the main road in alarm and careered towards a field. The second truck stopped and the people inside it ran off in all directions. Amongst them were many armed militia men. The second bomber also missed the mark.

— Look what the bastards are doing, - Said hissed through his teeth.

— They're lucky that the bombers were flying so fast that they missed their targets, - replied another lad whose name I didn't know.

The poor lad had tempted fate. As soon as the two bombers had flown off over our heads, two military helicopters appeared. They selected their targets and lined up before taking aim. The helicopters spat out of bullets like a threshing machine. The trucks were torn to pieces by the bullets and burst into flames. Their passengers had already run away. Fortunately, the helicopters did not fire at them but flew off towards Grozny.

— Let's go back or they could use us as targets too, - someone said, and we ran down the hill.

We stopped at the first house that we came across to drink some water, then we went to the road where the others were supposed to meet us. The instructor arrived towards evening. To my surprise, he was an Azerbaijani by the name of Ilgar. He explained that he had come to fight in our country. At that time the Azerbaijanis were thoroughly experienced in war. A few months before our war, they had ended their bloody battle with the Armenians for Nagorno-Karabakh. Lads from Azerbaijan were arriving in our country fully prepared for battle and well versed in the nuances of fighting against the Russians. In the Nagorno-Karabakh war the Armenians had fought under the watchful eyes of Russian officers.

The instructor said that the front line tapered towards Minutka Square. Other groups were putting up resistance in the Zavodskii district in the west. He assigned us to provide them with support.

– I have to go to the central hospital, - I said to Ilgar.

– As far as I know, that's right next to the Russian's headquarters. They have practically destroyed the hospital. You won't get within ten kilometres of it. And why do you need to go there? To collect a relative?

– I need morphine, that's why I came here. I have to get morphine and return to my village. They are waiting for me there, - I said.

Ilgar raised his eyebrows. Why had I travelled from one end of the country to the other, when I might have found morphine in my own district? I replied that I couldn't deprive the wounded of morphine. If I got it, it had to be from the hospital or from the Russians.

He called Said over and explained the situation to him. Said replied that my chances of survival if I went to the hospital were zero.

– The city is swarming with saboteurs. You won't get through alone and no-one will help you.

– It's all the same to me. I'll get through somehow.

– You decide. We'll try to reach Minutka and then you'll see for yourself, - said the instructor. He had other things to take care of.

And so it was agreed. We set off three hours before dawn. It was seven kilometres to Minutka. On the right-hand side of the road were open fields. They would be able to mow us down like partridges on these, so we decided to take the left-hand side, which was an area of dachas.

Ilgar ordered us to stop whenever he raised his hand. He was afraid of falling into a trap. Each time he stopped he looked through his night vision binoculars. Said was studying the sky above Grozny.

– Today the firing is less fierce than a couple of days ago, wouldn't you say so, Ilgar?

– Today it's relatively quiet, but the Russian silence is a bad sign. It means they will start bombing soon. Face to face fighting is not for them. When they see they can't take such-and-such a district they'll start to bomb it all day long, - Ilgar whispered in reply.

– When they bombed the area around the canning plant the sky lit up like on Victory Day. Everything blazed. Almost every soldier who was able to get out of there had burst eardrums and concussion - Said told us. The fighters had told him this in Shatoi.

The nearer we got, the louder the firing grew. In the distance I saw machine gun fire cutting through the sky.

– Those are tracer bullets - someone said. They are unstable. If they hit the body they don't pass through but start to spin. The chances of survival are minimal. Another minus is that when you fire them you have to constantly change your position as their fluorescence will give you away.

I did not know what kind of bullets I had, so I was unable to shoot at the enemy. When I saw another couple of tracer bullet tracks crossing over my head, I remembered a picture in a school textbook of Nero burning Rome. It was the famous story of how Nero burnt down part of the city inhabited by the poor so that he could observe the scene and describe it in one of his idiotic essays. Humanity has not changed one iota in two thousand years.

When the private plots of land came to an end we crossed an empty stretch of ground and reached a large military base. To our surprise we found a group of women hiding in the barracks. They worked in the nearby market that lay at a fork in the road that led from Argun and Shatoi, about two hundred metres from Minutka Square. They had been trading up to the last minute but the firing became so intense they were forced to retreat to the military base and wait before returning to the roadside when things had calmed down. They said that our troops were already in Minutka but there was a lot of firing going on. As dawn broke we saw how close the Russians were.

–   I can see a Russian tank... a second one is emerging, - said Ilgar, looking through his binoculars.

He held them out to me. I also saw a tank go by with a dozen soldiers walking behind it. But a sudden cry distracted my attention from the enemy. A man was approaching from the other side of the road, where apple orchards lay. Gasping for breath, he told us that at the entrance to the park their detachment had run into the enemy. The Russians had carried out a massacre of civilians. Under cover of night they had dug a common grave and thrown the bodies in. The stranger begged us for help, there was a battle taking place. We all raced after him.[17]

---

17 Abkhazia is a breakout region of Georgia, de-facto controled by Russian forces.

CHAPTER TWENTY SEVEN

Alexander uses Cunning to Capture Derbent

For many centuries before Derbent became the southern gateway to Russia it served as a northern outpost for the defence of the population along the whole Caspian Sea against invasion by wild tribespeople from the north. But by the time of Alexander their raids were devastating the region and Derbent soon fell under their onslaught. At this critical moment the great commander Alexander decided to help the people who lived along the Caspian shores. He led his 100,000 strong army towards the fortress.

In those times Derbent was small but very well defended with high fortified walls. Alexander decided there and then to take the fortress by using the full force of his soldiers and weaponry. His onslaught was so furious that by day the sun was blacked out by thousands of arrows. At night, thousands of balls of flame lit up the sky as brightly as the sun. Night took the place of day and day replaced night around the fortress. But its defenders stood firm. After a week of constant fire, Derbent remained unconquered.

– This town is prepared to fight to the death like an old maid fighting for her honour, - said Alexander, - And in both cases their sacrifice is unwarranted.

The furious efforts of the defenders to fight for the honour of the town only spurred on Alexander's desire to capture it. The Macedonian enquired whether there was a famous magician in the neighbourhood. He learned that there was one eccentric who ate only the roots of mountain grass, and who wove his clothes from the grass. He did not mix with people and for many years had seen no-one. People were not even sure that the man was still alive. Alexander decided to find the old man and ask him by what magic he could take Derbent.

The leader found the hermit in a deep cave into which the sun's rays never penetrated. This emaciated old man recognised his visitor.

– You know who I am? - asked the son of Philip[18] when they met.

– Well everyone recognises the moon at night, - the old man replied.

The magician's words went straight to Alexander's heart. In those days the rulers of the world must also have been susceptible to flattery. Getting straight to the point, he asked how he could seize the nearby fortress.

– I know many ways of capturing fortresses, but what are your true motives? Do you want the riches or Derbent or do you want to go down in history as the cleverest and most fearless military leader?

– One probably does not exclude the other, but above all I want to earn praise and honour for centuries to come.

– I'll tell you a tale about the contest between painters from China and from Rum[19] to find the best artist in the ancient world. This story will give you a hint about how to capture Derbent.

His interest aroused, Alexander began to listen to a story about how one day after a feast, the rulers of China and Greece decided to question whether the east or the west was the more developed in the fields of science, literature, art and so on. Each ruler began to praise the achievements of his own domain. The Chinese emperor said that the most powerful magicians on this earth came from India, to which the Greek ruler replied that every inhabitant of the earth is weak in comparison to the Arabs. The Chinese ruler praised Iraqi baths, the singers of Khorasan and the masons of Samarkand, while the Greek ruler lauded

18 Philip II of Macedon (382-336 BC) was Alexander the Great's father

19 Rum is the ancient Turkic name for Greece, used by Nizami

the odyssey of Homer. And so they quarrelled until morning, when one of the Greek king's viziers said.

– I'll be truthful. Only the painters of Rum are renowned.

– No, oh friend of painters, this is not true. There are artists in China, - said an aide who was standing behind the king.

So it was decided that the best artists of each country would paint a picture. Whoever painted the best picture would decide the question of whether the Occident or the Orient was more developed. They divided some thick material into two parts in order to form two studios. In each studio the artist would spend a few hours creating his greatest work. At the appointed time the curtain between the artists were drawn back to allow the judges to examine the pictures.

The judges gazed at the paintings and could not believe their eyes. The works of both artists were identical. The same decorative elements, colours and patterns. But how could it be that both pictures were absolutely identical, as the artists worked separately from each other and didn't know what the other was painting. The judges deliberated for a long while and couldn't find an explanation. But at that moment, as luck would have it, a fine rain began to fall. In order to protect the paintings they decided to wrap them in brocade. As soon as the Greek painter's work had been covered, in the blink of an eye the painting by the Chinese artist was also covered in the same brocade. How could that have happened? The painting by the Chinese artist was bewitched. It was not only identical to the Greek painting but covered in the same brocade.

As soon as the rain stopped the Chinese trick was uncovered. While the Greek artist was creating his chef-d'oeuvre, his opponent simply constructed a wall of shining lustre so that when the curtain was drawn back it faced the Greek painting. The polished wall reflected the painting like a mirror. One of the judges remarked.

– This artist gave birth to a picture so fine, but the other artist made it shine.

Therefore the judges decided that, because of the polish, Chinese art was the greatest of all.

The hermit's tale set Alexander thinking. But not for long. A moment later he sent his trusted soldiers into the Land of Darkness and there they bound up a sleeping horned monster like the one they had fought during the battle with the Russian tribes. They dragged the monster to Alexander's camp and at the same time Chinese masters made ready two huge mirrors. Towards morning they brought the monster bound in chains right to the fortress gates. The Chinese masters advised that one mirror should be placed near the monster's legs and the second mirror should stand straight and reflect the image of the monster. The Chinese knew that a mirror that reflects objects from below will make them seem larger than they are in reality.

One way or another, as morning broke, the defenders of Derbent saw the reflections of an enormous monster who was poised to attack them at any moment. They took it for a devil sent down from the heavens to help Alexander capture the fortress. In terror, they brought the key to the town to Alexander, and so after a long siege he captured Derbent in a few hours by using cunning. In his victory speech to his warriors, he said,

–   What is stronger than arrows, rocks and knives? I hope there will always be wise men alive.

The words of the great military leader resonated two thousand years later in the suburbs of Grozny, when the militia leaders cunningly enticed the Russians to the west. In this battle that killed dozens of Russian soldiers I would find the morphine that my father needed so badly.

CHAPTER TWENTY EIGHT

The Defenders of Grozny Show Their Cunning

After running for fifteen minutes we reached the entrance to the park. Among half-ruined, single-storey houses we heard the sounds of firing. The Russians had retreated to the right of us, and our forces were attacking from our left. Without even taking up positions we all opened fire. Now our units were firing from two directions the Russian soldiers were caught in crossfire. Two of the enemy soldiers fell dead.

When the Russians realised that they were trapped they ran into a small white house.

They'll sit it out there and defend themselves until help arrives, - shouted Ilgar. - They have a radio transmitter and those bastards in the tanks will race to their aid. We've got less than ten minutes to finish them off. Fire the grenade launchers, we haven't got much time.

We shelled the house. Flames blazed within as fire took hold, but the Russians went on firing in desperation. Our other group had no grenade launcher; theirs had been sent to the battles in the city, so we fired from our one launcher a few paces away from where I stood.

There was an infernal ringing in my ears. I lowered my head and clapped my hands against my ears to block out the noise. When I lifted my head again I saw two lads from the other detachment leaning against the walls of the house. How they managed to reach the house through the hail of bullets will remain a mystery to me. They threw in a couple of grenades. The firing from the house stopped. Ilgar glanced over at the road, fearing that the other detachment of Russians was coming to the aid of their comrades. Taking two of our men, he went around to the far side of the house. He probably wanted to check that the

Russians had not escaped through the back door. When I heard firing from that direction I realised that the Russians were trying to get out that way. Leaving the two men to guard the back exit, Ilgar returned.

– There are at least five or six still inside the house, - he said, - But they won't last long. Fire into the house all together. Don't spare the ammunition.

We obeyed. Soon the walls of the house looked like a sieve. The men from the other detachment gradually approached the house, firing point blank and throwing grenades inside. On our side the firing from the house had stopped. At that moment, Ilgar raised his bayonet so that the fighters from our other unit would see him. It was a signal that he was entering the house. He was armed only with a bayonet. I could see knives in three other hands. I didn't know then that some fighters had an unwritten custom. Enemy soldiers and officers who fell into their hands and who had shown particular savagery towards civilians – as was the case here - were slaughtered very cruelly. Our troops cut off their heads while still alive, or their genitals, and then they wrote messages in blood on the walls. And so, taking up his bayonet, Ilgar went over to the house and with two other men he jumped through the window into the burning building. We watched closely.

The minutes passed by very slowly. When they emerged again Ilgar showed me an ear he had cut from a Russian. He was very sorry that all the soldiers who had hidden in the house were dead when he entered it.

The most terrible sight awaited us when we reached the place where a pit had been dug and filled with corpses. There were many bodies of men, women and children. One boy of three or four years old had no trousers on, and I could see a bullet wound in his leg. Why had he been shot? What was he guilty of? Why had all the other children been killed? One of the dead women held a child tightly to her breast. She had probably tried to cover it with her body. I couldn't tear my eyes away from this monstrous sight. I would remember it forever. My eyes filled with tears. At that minute I could not have known that it was precisely this bloody atrocity that would save my life in the camp of the Arab, Al

Rashid. Hearing Arabic speech, I thought it must be a hallucination, but it was Said. He was reading a prayer. He struggled to pronounce the words, to squeeze them out through his constricted throat.

– Let's go, we have to re-join the others. We can't help these people, - said Said, after he had finished reading the yasin prayer which is read over the bodies of the fallen. I was still in shock.

We went back to the military base. A new group had assembled there. I didn't know where they had come from but, judging by their appearance they were exhausted. In their hands they held a small box.

– It is a surprise for the Russians, - said a young fighter, who looked more like a gypsy.

His face was all covered in dirt and his hair looked as though it had had clay rubbed into it. - We hit their helicopter tonight, three kilometres from here, - he continued. - And we took their emergency transmitter with us. They'll think the helicopter came down around here so we'll wait for them.

And so we waited, keeping watch on the sky and the city's outskirts where we had seen the tanks that morning. We camouflaged anti-aircraft guns behind the barracks. It was already midday when we saw the first military helicopter. We all ran through the barracks.

– And if they fire rockets at us, what will we do then? - I asked.

Said only shrugged. - We are in the hands of God.

I was afraid to come out of the barracks in case they would see us and fire on us. The lads who had arrived from town were already hardened fighters. Waiting for a minute while the helicopter made a couple of circles overhead, they began to fire as it approached. A short and incredibly loud burst of fire rang out, like a diesel generator. The base of the helicopter was hit and its propellers broke. The aircraft began to spiral from the sky. The pilot tried to direct the helicopter towards the side of the road that led towards Grozny. Their chances of survival would be better there, as they would fall among their own troops. But his attempt failed. We all ran towards the helicopter, firing at it as we ran. Not making it to the road, the aircraft hit the ground with a crash, nose first. Then its body slammed into the earth.

We began to fire again from a distance of around ten metres, aiming at the pilot's cabin.

—   Shall we approach it or not? - I asked the gunner who had brought down the helicopter.

Without replying, he ran forward, opened the door and looked inside.

—   There are medicines here! - he cried. Unable to believe my ears, I ran up to the helicopter and climbed in. It must have been carrying medicines to the crew of the other helicopter that our troops had brought down the night before. Grabbing some ampoules of morphine, I jumped out. I didn't want to push my luck. Others also took whatever they could lay their hands on, and ran off. For a long time I kept glancing behind me, expecting the helicopter to explode, but it went on standing there in proud isolation by the side of the road.

I was as happy as a child with my find. Now I could go back along the highway which we called the Road of Life. And it really was a road of life for me. Although later events would prove there was no cause to celebrate, we still believed that the tragedy unfolding in Chechnya would not spread beyond the borders of Grozny. But no, the Russians advancing towards Shatoi would surround and bombard all the villages along the way with artillery and tank fire. Fifty percent of Prigorodnoye was destroyed. Chechen-Aul, which consisted of around two thousand houses, was bombed to pieces. When a Government committee arrived a couple of years later to evaluate the damage, they declared that the remaining houses in the village were unfit for human habitation. If the shells hadn't hit them, then bombs exploding nearby had rendered them too unstable for use.

And another terrible tragedy was the mass shooting of civilians on the Shatoi-Grozny road, at the crossing with the Baku-Rostov highway. The Russians set up a post on either side of the road. When the soldiers, having finished their task, returned to Grozny they shot dozens of unarmed civilians, including women and children, on the way. No-one knows precisely how many innocent people died there.

CHAPTER TWENTY NINE

Zalimkhan the Healer

Late in the evening and deathly tired, I opened the gate of our house and went inside. My parents were waiting for me. I entered my father's room. Abdulaziz was sitting lost in thought; he seemed more exhausted than I was. His eyes met mine, not with that look of censure, reproach or disappointment that he used to give me when I had done something stupid in childhood. No, he looked at me with eyes of a doomed man. At that moment I hated everything in this world. I was relieved when my mother struggled to her feet and asked if I was hungry. I had not had any proper food for many days now.

— What's going on in Grozny now? What are they saying down there? - my father asked.

— Grozny is already in the hands of the Russians. They are battling for the Oktyabr district right now, and they'll take it soon. Our fighters have withdrawn to the mountains. We have to recoup our forces and from summer we'll launch another attack on the city.

— They won't give us time to recover. In summer, when they open the roads, the Russians will reach our village. They'll bomb us with artillery and from helicopters, and then we'll flee to Georgia as our ancestors did a hundred and fifty years ago, - he said.

— Father, the Russians won't defeat us. They've already lost five thousand of their best soldiers in Grozny. The lads who are replacing them have never even smelled gunpowder; they've never seen blood in their lives. While we've seen so much damned blood since childhood. As kids we took knives in our hands to slaughter sheep, cows and wild game. The Russians faint at the sight of blood. Their commanders have to force them into battle. They give them ancient guns and sell the new weapons for dollars. Sometimes they even sell their own soldiers, - my voice was sharp.

I was on fire. Hundreds of our lads were dying for the Motherland, displaying true heroism, and again my father was making his pessimistic forecasts.

— Justice is on our side, courage is on our side, and Allah is on our side. If there is any justice in this world, then we'll drive all those Russians out of our towns like mangy curs, - I ranted.

— If there is any justice, then we shall win, - Abdulaziz murmured, and made a sign that I should leave the room. His gesture was unnecessary. I did not want to quarrel with him any longer. I was afraid of going too far.

My mother was sitting at the table which was laid with food.

— Go easy on your father, he doesn't sleep at night, his nerves are in shreds. If he's lucky, he'll drop off for half an hour and then the pain will wake him again. How he can bear it I don't understand. May Allah have mercy upon him, - she said as I chewed a drumstick with relish. Then I threw myself on what remained of the chicken and, without finishing it, I picked up some bread, cheese and a piece of sausage. I ate everything my mother put before me, even forgetting that you shouldn't eat sausage with chicken. I'd never done that before.

— It will get harder and harder, mother, - I said, chewing the last piece of bread. Morphine is no longer helping father, he is wasting away before our eyes.

— But Allah loves him, He'll help us. We have to believe in His power. Then she said something I didn't quite understand.

I didn't have the strength to listen to such words from my mother. I was trying to talk to her about concrete problems and she answered with empty platitudes.

It just wasn't my day. I was wound up and prepared for an argument. "I'd better go to bed before I say anything stupid," I said to myself, and went to my room.

In the morning I understood what supernatural power my mother was talking about - she had a trick up her sleeve.

In my father's room I found a bearded stranger. He was holding my father's arm and rubbing some glutinous mixture on it. It was the colour of nettles and stank horribly. I don't know what it was - probably some herbs cooked up together, or a mixture of chemicals.

–   This is Zalimkhan the Healer. He's a refugee from the Grozny region and is
    staying in our village for a while. He is a man of God and has already helped
    many of our neighbours, - my mother proudly announced.

"Here we go again. God, what have I done to deserve this?" I said to myself, shaking my head in annoyance. No-one knew who this Zalimkhan was, or what he did, or what kind of education he'd had. I didn't believe in these charlatans. Most of them were rogues without any fixed line of work. In order to feed themselves these so-called healers wandered around the country just as travelling cinemas once did. That's why I was scowling. But what shocked me most of all was that my father also believed in this Zalimkhan. After the healer had covered his arm in this mysterious paste, my mother brought a bandage and bound it up. Zalimkhan told us to leave the arm for two hours without touching it and then wash everything off. Later he would put the paste on for a second time.

–   Zalimkhan doesn't take money for his treatments. If the patient recovers
    then we can give him a gift. But no more than that. He is sent by God. He
    will save Father, you'll see, - my mother went on trying to convince me.

Zalimkhan stood up to leave and to my surprise my father also got to his feet to see him out. I hastened to support Abdulaziz and help him out onto the veranda. Giving a couple more words of advice, Zalimkhan left. My father was in a good mood and asked my mother to bring his jacket. He wanted to walk around the garden. I couldn't believe my eyes.

– He is an astonishing person, very educated and honest. His strength lies in his faith. You meet few people like that these days, - said my father.

Zalimkhan returned in exactly two hours. He took off the bandage and again applied this mysterious embrocation to my father's arm.

– God willing, your arm will slowly but surely recover. I mixed drooping alfredia and broad-leaved gentian with ordinary fat. This will restore the tissue in the arm. In a couple of weeks you'll see how the colour of your arm will change and take on a more healthy tone.

Abdulaziz bowed his head in acknowledgement. Then the two men sat down to discuss many things, the power of faith, the period when Bukhara, Samarkand, Khiva and other central Asian cities flourished, and why that great heritage was never resurrected after the devastating invasions of Genghis Khan. And then they discussed the mysteries of the South American and Egyptian pyramids.

– What did the Almighty say in the Quran about the power of faith? - Zalimkhan began, - "And set your hopes on the living one who does not die."

– It was the same with the prophet Abraham. When they tried to burn him he said, "We need only Allah, our protector". They bound him head and foot and threw him into the flames but he survived, - my father added.

The Healer listened attentively. His expression spoke of his respect for my father. Zalimkhan never interrupted him. When he wanted to say something he laid his hand on my father's arm as if to ask for permission to speak.- If you study history from the time of Alexander, then you will see that unconditional faith was the most important source of victory. It was neither intelligence nor military skill, but strong faith which drew forth the talents of military leaders, - said the healer.

Zalimkhan said that Alexander the Great had been motivated by faith in his own uniqueness, Spartacus by a desire for freedom and Hannibal by hatred of the Romans. All these feelings were elevated to the highest level, on a par with religious faith.

My mother brought in tea, and rice mixed with raisins. It was our local delicacy.

— Why are Caucasian fighters the best in the world? It is not because we have strong characters and a classical school of combat, but because most of our boys believe in Allah; it gives them an immeasurable strength which is lacking in our opponents, - Zalimkhan concluded.

It was impossible to argue with him. I know that from personal experience I was also driven by belief – belief in the need to save my father. The conversation flowed smoothly on to the subject of Central Asia, to their painters, ceramicists, metal workers and other masters. The two men spoke about the types of figurative form in the art of Asia and Arabia, and the reason for the decline of science and art in the later periods of the Khorezm and Samanid empires. I was astounded by the Healer's thinking. He said that after the invasions of Genghis Khan the ancient empires of Central Asia could not regain their glory for a long time, and this was all because they did not grant the artistic and creative freedoms that had previously been the norm.

— Freedom has no measure, but that does not diminish its significance. The Christians understood this before us, and we can see the results, - my father said.

— That's right, they don't fight each other any more. That time passed fifty years ago. Now they only conquer by means of culture - the healer agreed.

After talking for four hours, Zalimkhan left. My mother was overjoyed. She had to give my father an injection so I left the room. When I reached the door my mother began to call for me. "What now?" I fretted.

143

— Bring a small bucket from the kitchen, run, - she shouted from the doorway. Without understanding why it was needed, I hurriedly obeyed.

She wouldn't let me into the room. Half an hour later she emerged with the bucket, half-full with pus. Seeing the surprise on my face, she said that a month ago a cavity had formed in the place where she gave the injections and it had begun to fill up with who knew what. Today when she gave the injection, the swelling burst and pus flowed out, mixed with thick blood.

Ayna believed that this was Zalimkhan's doing. I too began to have a bit more faith in him. The next morning Abdulaziz really did feel better.

— If this continues, then in two weeks' time we'll be able to celebrate his birthday properly, - my mother said in a bright voice. - You see, he will recover, - she assured me.

CHAPTER THIRTY

Baku

In 24 hours I reached the Azerbaijan border at a place called SDK. I had to pass many checkpoints set up along the Baku-Rostov highway. From Shali, Kurcheloi, Khasavyurt to the border there were seven checkpoints where you had to pay a minimum of twenty roubles. And if you were a young man then you paid several times more. There was chaos at the border, too. For a bribe, the Russians were letting people and cars through. I gave money and my passport to a local Dagestani, and he took them to the official's booth together with the documents of two other Chechens.

— You can travel to Baku together, - he said, handing me back my passport.

— And where are they, those Chechens?

— In a goods lorry.

A nondescript truck was parked nearby. Inside were two wounded Chechens lying on stretchers, and a young man who was looking after them.

— After you've crossed the border, an ambulance will meet us and take you to Baku, - he said in a serious tone.

We crossed the border without being stopped. Just as the young man said, there were ambulances waiting on the other side, with doctors in them. They had a quick look at the wounded and then we set off towards Baku. We scarcely spoke along the way. The doctors briefly told me that the injured were from western Chechnya, from the village of Semashka. They had brought them across the entire country to Azerbaijan. I had heard nothing about that village until then. At the beginning of April, interior ministry troops had "cleansed" the village

145

and killed more than a hundred people, of whom no more than a few were resistance fighters. In three hours we reached the city of Baku. After another twenty minutes of driving through unfamiliar streets we reached a hospital. An old sign with cracked glass announced that this was 'Hospital Number 5.'

Grasping one end of the stretcher, I helped to unload the wounded soldiers and take them into the hospital. Only then did I realise the scale of the tragedy that had taken place in Chechnya. Inside the building I saw one of our fighters lying in the corridor beneath a woollen blanket. His face was very pale. I went up to a nurse and asked her where I might find Doctor Samir Lyutvaliev.

–   You're going the wrong way. Turn round and go up the stairs to the first floor, - she said, pushing me away from the injured fighter. - If he picks up the slightest infection, he will not survive. Go on, get out of here, - she barked.

–   We have as many wounded now as we had during the war in Nagorno-Karabakh. We haven't enough time to operate as the wounded keep pouring over the border, - Samir said to me after I explained how I had come to find him. That instructor, Ilgar, had given me his details so that I wouldn't have to go to Grozny when our morphine ran out. Samir went on to tell me about his friendship with the instructor.

–   Ilgar, Vagit and I were childhood friends. When the war began, Ilgar and Vagit went to fight in Karabakh. God looked after them but in the summer of 1993 our troops took part in a massive advance to the edge of Khankendi. There on the roof of the PTU building, Vagit was killed. The Armenians launched a heavy attack on that building. If it hadn't have been for the Chechens beside him, Ilgar would not have been able to take Vagit's body out and bury him according to our traditions, - said Samir in a calm voice.

–   The war in Karabakh was a bleeding wound for Azerbaijan. Thirty thousand soldiers and officers died there. With the support of Russia, the Armenians seized villages, towns and whole districts, wiping out the civilian population.

In Khodjaly alone, they slaughtered six hundred civilians. The cruelty of the Armenians in Khodjaly may be compared to that of the Serbs in Srebrenica. Both there and in Karabakh the same system for wiping out the civilian population was used; surrounding the town on all sides, forming a supposed corridor and killing them as they passed through this corridor.

The evenness of Samir's tone as he described the tragic Karabakh war struck me as strange. He went on in a similarly calm voice to tell me how they had brought his friend's body to Baku, how all Vagit's friends and relatives assembled, and how they carried his body along Shakhidov Road in the centre of town and buried him with honours. Samir related the story of his friend's death as though he were telling a fairy story, without emotion or exclamation. At first I thought this might be something to do with his profession. Doctors usually have a different attitude to death, life, pain and suffering as a whole, although there was one 'but,' and that was Samir's eyes. I have never seen such honesty, depth and sincerity in anyone's eyes. They were the eyes of an honest person, a man of honour. I wondered how he could be so restrained as he described the death of his friend, but it was impossible to believe that he didn't suffer over it. His eyes gave him away.

Our conversation was very brief. I told him what I needed. He found four boxes of morphine and gave them to me. I did not offer him money for them. Before he was called to go downstairs, Samir said that I could come to him at any time if I needed anything. I left the hospital in a lighter mood. I had a good supply of morphine now. I decided to return home via Georgia. I would have to cross the border and go from Rustavi to Lagodekhi and from there across the border at the Pankisi Gorge, and then return home. Before I went to the coach station I decided to have a look at Baku. Hailing a taxi, I asked to be taken to the centre. Taxis in Baku were very strange. They were yellow, and certainly not of Russian make. The driver said that the cars are imported from Turkey. They even have air-conditioning.

– I have sat behind the wheel for thirty years, - the elderly driver enthused, - And until now, I never knew that you could put air-conditioning into cars. So in summer, when it reaches forty degrees, my clients will be in seventh heaven.

The old man asked me to close the window on my side. He turned a switch beside the cassette recorder. Fresh air blew through the car. In a couple of minutes it became quite cool and pleasant. - You see! - he said happily.

Five-storey buildings flashed by and then smaller two or three-storey houses surrounded by lovely gardens. "Oh Lord, once Grozny was as beautiful as this. Now there are only ruins and graveyards full of wrecked human lives," I thought to myself.

The buildings grew taller and grander and the roads widened. I realised we were driving through the central part of the city.

– You should begin your tour here, - said my cheerful driver.

I alighted in front of some kind of park beside the sea. I was on the famous Baku Boulevard. My father had sometimes spoken about it, saying it was the largest promenade that he had ever seen in his life. Here I would be able to see the beauty of Baku. On the opposite side of the road stood the splendid palaces of oil magnates, confiscated by the Bolsheviks after the October Revolution. The oil millionaires of Azerbaijan had not only been rich but also great philanthropists, the flowers of the nation. They spent huge sums of their personal wealth on building high schools for girls, children's homes, theatres and concert halls. Such buildings filled the city centre.

I fell in love with Baku because of the sea, which I was seeing for the first time in my life. The Caspian Sea gently welcomed its visitors with fresh breezes which filled the streets with the scent of fish and oil, at least these were the smells that I picked up as I walked along the boulevard. The Boulevard itself had seen better days. Its beauty consisted of aging seafront attractions with paint peeling from them, potholed asphalt, a huge boat named "Turkmenistan" and a couple of grandmothers selling sunflower seeds and photographs.

Crossing through an underpass, I emerged in a square surrounded by gracious five-storey buildings. A hundred metres further on I glimpsed the ancient walls of the old city. A narrow cobblestoned street led up to them. Walking up this street, by the happiest of coincidences I came upon a huge statue of Nizami. The handsome poet in a turban proudly stared into space. Allah loved Nizami so much that he gave him everything - beauty, phenomenal talent, intelligence and the moral principles which he was faithful to until the end of his life. All these features had been skillfully conveyed by the sculptor.

Circling the monument, I saw two huge and ancient arches leading to the old city. These must have been the main entrance to the fortress. Whatever they had been, I was more attracted by two lions engraved over the arches. They reminded me of the statue of lions in the cave of the legendary Persian King Kei Khosrov that I had read about in Iskandername, the book of Alexander. "Perhaps this is the entrance to the Kei Khosrov cave which disappeared so many centuries ago," I said to myself. I was intrigued. Some unknown force drew me towards them.

The old town was crammed with single-storey houses whose windows were protected by iron grilles. Here and there minarets rose up and there were some souvenir stalls for tourists. The narrow streets somehow reminded me of the Persian Shah's cave, although there was not a trace of burning rivers of sulphur. Continuing my path along the walls, after ten minutes I emerged at another great arch which had huge metal doors. Alongside it, gathered by the wall, stood some Chechens. I recognised them by their traditional headdress. It turned out that this was the centre for aid for Chechen refugees. I went up and introduced myself. Among them were many people wearing bandages. One man had a large piece of bloodied yellow flesh hanging from his arm. He said that he had been injured by fragments from a bomb filled with chemicals that had been dropped on Grozny.

- There are many puddles in the city of a strange brown colour, - he said. - These are pools of chemicals that collected after rocket attacks. The rockets contained chemical substances. We have to tell people to avoid these puddles.

- And what do the doctors here say? - I asked sympathetically.

– They don't even know what I have been infected by. They said I should seek help at a military hospital. And so I wait, killing time in Baku. Otherwise, I'd go somewhere else.

The aid centre was a small two-roomed building. Inside there was a queue, or rather a queue in each room. In the first there were mainly women receiving rice, oil, flour and other necessities. In the second there was a suspicious silence. Mistakenly I thought that they might be giving out arms in there. The thought had just crossed my mind when the sound of a struggle and cries dispelled my suspicions. A second later a young man, clutching his nose from which blood trickled, ran out of the room.

The waiting people soon told me what had happened. In that ill-fated room a representative of the UN Refugee Council was drawing up a list of Chechen refugees in Baku. To his misfortune, the young UN employee called one of our fighters a refugee. The Chechen could not restrain himself and punched the UN worker in the face, saying, - A Highlander cannot be a refugee.

The poor lad, he was only trying to do his job and he got hit. In his own country too. It was not right, but I also understood the guy who started the fight. The words "Highlander" and "refugee" do not equate.

By evening I was at the coach station. I climbed aboard an old Icarus bus smelling of sweat and cheap cigarette smoke. It set off for Ganja in the west of Azerbaijan. After five hours on the road contemplating the flat landscape of the countryside, we reached the outskirts of the city. But I was not destined to see it, for I forgot everything else in the world when I caught sight of the huge marble burial vault of Nizami on the edge of Ganja. It was hard to believe that his grave had been preserved for eight hundred years after his death.

It was a huge monument, at least twenty metres high - the tallest I had seen in my life - built of black marble. Behind the monument was a large park with statues of Nizami's heroes. There was Alexander the Great, proudly seated on his horse. The square in front of Nizami's tomb was packed with foreigners of some European country or other. To the side, near a flower bed, sat the lone figure of an old man in worn out shoes and coat. He looked very shabby and I thought he was homeless or a beggar asking for alms.

As I drew closer to the guide I heard he was speaking Russian. It turned out that the tourists who I had taken for Europeans were musicians in an Estonian symphony orchestra. It was really all the same to me where they came from. I was only interested in going inside the poet's mausoleum, so I spent a few minutes mingling with the Estonians. Together with my Baltic brothers and sisters, we listened to the guide. After a couple of minutes he invited us to ascend the staircase around the burial vault. The stairs led not to the burial chamber itself, but to a surrounding balcony from which, if you lent over a little, you could see the poet's grave.

– There in this grave, covered in white marble, lies the great poet, - the guide said. - For the past eight hundred years, Ganja has suffered much tragedy: war; severe earthquakes; epidemics that killed thousands of people. The only thing that has remained unchanged is the grave of Nizami Ganjavi. The town's citizens preserve it as a holy site.

I wanted to look at the poet's grave more closely, but for that I had to lean forward. From where I was standing I could only see the white marble headstone. Trying as hard as I could to view the whole grave, I bent still further forward.

Seeing my discomfort, the guide said, - It was specially built like that. The nearer you get to the tomb, the lower you have to bow down before Nizami.

– It was cleverly thought out, - I replied with a smile. "I have already bowed down before him, a long while before I came here," I thought to myself.

– Are you from Estonia too? - asked the guide.

– No, I'm from Chechnya, - I replied

No sooner had I spoken the words than my Estonian comrades began to ply me with questions about the current situation in the Republic, about the war and the battle for Grozny. In short, they wanted to know everything. Open-mouthed, the Estonians hung on to my every word, rejoicing like children when I told them about our successes, and showing genuine sadness when they heard what the Russians had done in Chechnya as a whole. In a few minutes it felt as though I was part of their family. They were going on to make a tour of Georgia and asked if I would like to travel with them free of charge. I agreed. When we emerged from the mausoleum, the old man I had seen earlier approached us, asking for alms. He had happened to overhear our conversation, so he also knew I was from Chechnya. Taking my arm, he led me aside to a place from which we could see the ruined castle walls of Ganja.

—   You won't find many cities whose fates have resembled each other so closely as Ganja and Grozny, - he said, indicating the remains of the high city walls.

"The old boy is probably a bit touched," I thought. But I was wrong. He told me things that I would never have expected to hear from a beggar. First, that the Chechen war was linked to Russia's expansionist aims in Azerbaijan and Georgia. After installing a puppet regime in Armenia, taking Georgia and Azerbaijan would restore Russian rule in the southern Caucasus. And then war in Chechnya began, which was to use up all Russia's human and military resources. Second, the beggar said that in 1803 in Ganja, the Russians did exactly what they are doing now in Grozny. One and the same scenario, one and the same method. In those days the local ruler, Javad Khan, refused to surrender the fortress to the Russian General Tsitsianov without a battle. This all took place when the separate kingdoms in the Caucasus became subjects of the Russian empire. Georgia, the northern khanates and principalities, and the khanate of Azerbaijan were among the last territories to be conquered. When this "proposal" was made to Javad Khan of Ganja, he answered very simply, - I am not your vassal. If you want war then we are ready.

—   And so, just as in Grozny on the first days of January, the Russians invaded under cover of night. After several days' fighting, the soldiers of Tsitsianov killed Javad Khan and one of his sons. And the Khan's little grandson was slashed to pieces with a sabre as he lay in his cradle. During the seizure of Ganja fifteen hundred of the Khan's followers were killed and seventeen thousand taken prisoner. The Khan's beautiful palace was plundered and looted, and for a long time the building was used as a barracks for Russian troops. Then, just like in Grozny today, people fought for every building, for every street. It was a real battle, - said the old man.

– The city's name was changed to Elizavetopol, in honour of the Empress Elizabeth. But the local residents refused to use the city's new name, so the authorities introduced a fine. Whoever called the city by its old name would be fined one silver rouble. But that didn't help; the locals paid their fines to the exchequer in advance, and then went out into the main square and shouted out the old name.

– In this life what goes around comes around. The Russian General did not enjoy the fruits of his victory for long. Three years later, in 1804, during an attempt to take Baku, its ruler, Huseyngulu cut Tsitsianov's throat and sent his head to the ruler of Iran as a gift.

The beggar's tale turned my thoughts back to Grozny. I thought of Ruslan, of whom I had had no news, the woman at Shtoum-Kale who went out of her mind after losing her children in Grozny, and the dead child shot through the legs lying beside his mother. I knew these memories would remain with me for the rest of my life. These thoughts depressed me and my head began to ache from tension. My suffering probably showed in my face, and the old man tried to dispel my sad thoughts by asking me questions about myself.

– What are you doing so far from home, son? - he asked.

– I am a reader of Nizami. I spoke quietly so that no-one else could hear my reply. In those days I believed that a true Highlander should not read poetry. "For that's what weaklings do," I thought.

153

— I am a beggar, - the old man continued. – Only two things keep me alive. The neighbours who feed me and Nizami, who helps me to survive on the moral level.

And here I was thinking I was the only fool to be enraptured by Nizami. It turns out that there are other people on this earth who are just like my father and me.

— When I leaf through 'Khosrov and Shirin', I remember how I fought for my love. When I read 'Leyli and Majnun', I remember my happy family life. 'Iskandername' inspires me to fight and not give up. When I read Nizami, I receive so much positive energy, so much peace, that I can withstand any amount of cold or hunger.

— It's the same with me, - I replied, struck by the old man's sincerity. - I am reading 'Iskandername'.

The old man interrupted me. - You know that Nizami wrote poetry for you and me? Precisely for you and me. For all who are standing before his grave right now. Even for those Estonians who cannot understand the greatness of Nizami, - he said, as he began to leaf through his book. - It's a very short poem, but it will touch every cell of your body, every capillary, every artery. Just listen carefully.

Then the old man read a short poem. It struck me so forcefully that I memorised it on the spot. At that moment, Nizami's soul touched mine. It even seemed to me that I could hear his quiet and calm voice. Listen carefully:

> O young friend, by my weathered grave,
> Stand in silence and remember my name.
> See how my tombstone has collapsed,
> How grass grows tall between the slabs.
> Scatter my ashes; not one of my friends
> Has been to my grave for years on end.
> Touch this gloomy tomb my son,

And think upon the soul that's gone.
But I once lived as thou dost now,
And so I long to inspire thy soul.
Do not believe thou art here alone,
I see thee, but thou seest only stone.
Remember this: I am always beside thee,
And noble deeds will be thine – trust in me.

I have done a noble deed. I saved my father and all the while Nizami was with me. How could he foresee that eight hundred years after his death a young Highlander, whose father was dying, would come to his grave? And how this young man would overcome all his difficulties through reading his book? And how he would become the spiritual father of this young man who would be lost without his work?

I reached Tbilisi with the Estonians. I could have gone straight to Rustavi and from there through the Pankisi Gorge back to my village. But I wanted to take this opportunity to see Tbilisi. My first impressions were very painful. As we travelled along the banks of the River Kuri, I saw rows of gloomy nine-storey blocks with the flues of home-made stoves sticking out of their windows. Electricity only worked for a few hours a day and people needed to heat their flats and cook food. The whole journey into the centre of the city revealed the poverty and dejection that had descended on Georgia. The streets were full of ancient battered cars of foreign make and little markets selling a jumble of goods.

I already regretted my decision to come to Tbilisi but my low spirits lifted a little on Rustaveli Street. Here in the city's main thoroughfare I began to see, understand and even taste the true Georgia. Handsome young people: lads dressed cheaply but smartly and girls in multi-coloured scarves walked along Rustaveli with heads held high as though they lived in Paris itself. In an underpass near the Conservatoire I came upon a bunch of wandering musicians lustily singing in English. The Georgians' behaviour and appearance announced to the world that all their current difficulties were merely temporary and soon everything would change for the better. Then the good life would begin.

Modern Tbilisi reminded me of the decline of Rome, which we had learned about in Aïsha Rasulova's history lessons. One of the richest cities of the USSR, a great administrative and cultural centre lay in ruins, but the poor citizens still believed in the greatness of their city, the greatness which it deserved but which had been taken from it by the force of circumstance.

After eating an Adzharian khatchapuri - delicious warm bread with Uzbek melon and egg in the middle, I travelled towards the Akhmedski district. From there, I went through the Pankisi Gorge, and in another day I was back at home.

CHAPTER THIRTY ONE

Alexander and the Cave of the Legendary Khosrov

For several thousand years before the fame of Alexander the Great cast its shadow over the minds of future generations, in the ancient world there existed a cult of the Persian king, Kei Khosrov. He was regarded as a model of military valour, justice and might. In the sixty years of his reign Khosrov founded the vast Persian Empire, much larger than that of the later king, Darius. He destroyed the temple of idols on Lake Urmia, built the fortress of Kangdezi with fifteen gates, where it took fifteen days on horseback to ride from one to the other and where it was always spring. And throughout his life he fought with the Turkish tribes. It is interesting that 'Khosrov and Shirin,' the epic tale of the love between the king Khosrov and the Turkish princess, Shirin, is considered to be Nizami's best work.

No-one knew where Khosrov was buried. According to legend, at the peak of his glory he renounced his throne and went to live as a hermit in a cave in the Caucasus, and there he died. Those who came after him believed that whoever found his tomb and read the writing on the golden cup, which symbolised power, would know the secrets of the Persian ruler's success.

— I'll behold the tomb and strengthen my soul; thereafter nothing will thwart my rule, - said Alexander to his friend, Bulinas, when he decided to find Khosrov's cave.

He searched for almost a month. Finally, near the castle of Sirar, which lies at one end of the great Caucasian range on the territory of modern Azerbaijan, he found the cave of the great king. Or rather, he found what was left of it. In Khosrov's time it had been reached by a narrow winding road but now this was destroyed, leaving only the spectacular entrance to the cave, which was formed like the open jaws of a lion on the bare cliff face.

— How would you advise us to climb the cliff face, oh trusted Bulinas? - Alexander asked.

— We have to find a local and ask them the way inside, - his warrior replied.

So they sent a soldier to the fortress of Sirar to find out more about the secret cave. However, having found out that the great Alexander was near the fortress, the commander of Sirar ran over to bow down before him. But his ensuing advice only seemed to make matters worse.

— Great leader, - the warrior said. - Since Kei Khosrov was interred in the cave many centuries ago, no-one has been able to enter it. The narrow road that led to the entrance disappeared overnight. How it was lost, no-one knows. But there is something even more horrifying. Demons live in the cave of the great Khosrov, guarding his tomb.

— What kind of demons? And who's seen them? - Alexander questioned him.

— Well it would not be true to say we have actually seen them, but we certainly hear them every night. As soon as the moon lights the sky, the cave starts to blaze with fire and the fearsome howls and cries of the demons terrify everyone in the fortress. The demons hurl fire at each other as they fight to the death. And they devour anyone who goes near, - said the warrior, glancing at the cave in fear.

— How many people have tried to reach the king's tomb? - the leader insisted heatedly.

— No-one in our times, but several centuries ago they say there were such bold spirits. What became of them, no-one knows. Some say they were eaten by the demons, others say that their groans can still be heard at night. Nowadays people avoid that accursed place.

Alexander had experienced so much in his life, he had fought so many battles and won so many victories, that exploring the cave seemed like an after-dinner stroll to him. In a firm but ironic tone, he ordered,

— Let the troops have a good sleep. This evening we shall see with our own eyes what kind of dark forces are disporting themselves in that mysterious hole.

Sure enough, when darkness fell, the cave began to glow. A blaze of light shone from the lion's jaws. It seem as though something within the cave was breathing flames through the beast's mouth. It would pause, and after another ten minutes breathe out flames again. It made a noise like a leopard's roar. And then, as the soldiers stared up at the cliff, they saw shadows of unknown creatures dancing in wild ecstasy, mingling with one another in outlandish postures. This whole devilish spectacle invoked terror in Alexander's troops.

Morning found his soldiers in a terrible state of mind. They moaned that no-one would emerge alive from the cave, that they were warriors accustomed to fighting and dying on the field of battle. They were not prepared to be devoured by unknown creatures. "With my soldiers wavering like this, I might as well give up without a fight," Alexander thought to himself.

— Soldiers! - he roared. - We have seen monsters and worse. Remember the huge monster we defeated in Abkhazia, the many months of our expedition to the Land of Darkness, and our countless other trials? Our enemies then were visible, terrifying, powerful and ferocious. And what of it? Only my faith in you and your faith in me saved us from death. And it will be the same now.

Alexander paused and looked straight into the eyes of his faithful warriors.

— The words of the alchemist may be gloomy forsooth, but there is no need to mistake them for truth, - he concluded.

– Glory to Alexander! Glory to Alexander the Great! - the soldiers cheered. In two hours they stood covered in sweat and dust at the top of the cliff, ready to lower ropes down to the cave. Alexander and Bulinas were the first to descend. The derelict entranceway was covered in spiders' webs and an unpleasant smell disturbed the two men.

– Where are the demons? Perhaps they have taken fright and hidden themselves.

– Perhaps the godless ones have laid a trap, - Bulinas replied.

The deeper Alexander went into the cave, the worse the smell became. Soon the passageway began to narrow and the ceiling of the cave grew lower. With a burning torch in his hand the great leader went ahead and his soldiers followed him. Soon they had to advance on all fours. Finally they emerged into a vast space. It was the most beautiful chamber Alexander had ever seen. A mysterious crimson river ran over a bed of granite, and in the centre of the cavern stood Khosrov's golden throne surrounded by tall pillars of elephant bones and hundreds of gold and silver adornments. And there was the Persian king's enormous golden chalice, the symbol of his power.

First of all, one of the commander's wise men lowered himself on a rope to the mysterious crimson river. The river was viscous; bubbles erupted into blinding flares of a strange brilliance. When he returned, the wise man said that the inner chamber was ablaze with the type of flame that scholars would identify as sulphur.

– Sulphur fills the air, it stifles and burns all those who come near, - the wise man said.

And so the secret of the night-time demons was revealed. Bubbles of sulphur swelled and burst, releasing flames. The shadows of the bursting bubbles appeared to the citizens of Sirar as cavorting demons, and the energy released by the bubbles seemed to be a dragon breathing fire.

What were they to do next? Part of the secret of the cave of Kei Khosrov was revealed. Now they had to uncover a second, more important, mystery - the secret power of the Persian king's throne and chalice. And so Alexander decided to cross the river of sulphur. Forming a bridge from ropes, he managed to reach the centre of the chamber and mounted Khosrov's throne. Despite the grandeur and elegance of the throne, with its vast number of inlaid emeralds and diamonds, it felt cold and uncomfortable. It was as though the throne had been built for Khosrov alone to sit on. Examining the king's chalice, Alexander read the following lines.

'Why preserve this throne of gold, for another king to make his own?'

It meant that Khosrov had hidden his throne so that no-one else would find it. No one except he would be able to boast of his attributes, acquired through blood and will power. Realising this, Alexander ordered the entire burial chamber of Khosrov to be destroyed ...

... Closing the book, I reflected for a moment. Reason and logic told me that Alexander could have acted differently. Why destroy that which you have fought so hard to attain? Because if you strive for something with all your might, you should be equally rewarded. Where the justice lies in this, the devil alone knows. Why then do we convince ourselves to do all that lies within our powers so that Allah will reward us?

For the first time since I had opened the book on Alexander, I regretted that I had begun to read Nizami. The book had given me hope, had held out an unseen hand, had inspired me when I was in a state of despair and one step away from death. For me, all Alexander's victories over the Russians, the wild northern tribes, his journeys in the land of Darkness, and the cave of Kei Khosrov were more significant than the parting blessings of kinfolk and the sincere wishes of friends. Nothing motivated me or protected me from harm as much as this history written eight hundred and fifty years ago.

But now I was upset. What did Nizami mean to tell me by this last deed of Alexander? As hard as I tried I could not work out how to reconcile myself with this tale. I might as well try to reach the moon. For some reason Nizami, my unseen teacher, had decided to deliver a shock at the point where the story reached its climax. Undoubtedly only he knows the truth of the matter.

CHAPTER THIRTY TWO

Death

On arriving home I found everything plunged into gloom. Death was waiting in the wings. My father lay unconscious, my mother was sleeping in her room, overcome by exhaustion. The stench of death pervaded the house - that smell which I could distinguish from a thousand other smells. I loathed it beyond the point of endurance. I opened the windows so that the breeze could carry away the stench and the gloom, but it clung on. I decided to do whatever I could to drive that damn smell from the house.

"Perhaps it comes from my father and I need to wash him," I thought to myself. Hurrying into the yard, I lit a fire and put water on to heat. When it was ready I filled a bucket and went into my father's room. He was sleeping face down. No, he was not asleep, he had lain unconscious for three days in the same nightclothes without regaining consciousness. He was as thin as a skeleton and his skin was a yellowish colour.

What has this illness done to him? How has it tortured this proud human being? When I was little I thought my father was brave and immortal, and now he lies before me in his ravaged body. Wetting a cloth, I began to wipe his arms and legs. The hideous stench filled my nostrils but I went on rubbing his skin, removing pellets of dirt. Abdulaziz showed no signs of life. Having cleaned his arms and legs, I turned to his body. Putting my hand beneath his nightshirt, I started to wash his chest. His heart was very weak but it was beating. At that moment I recalled Dr Mohammed's words, - You must realise that if he has a strong heart his death will be protracted and terrible. Right now his heart kept his whole body clinging to life. In half an hour he was clean. Nevertheless, the smell of death remained in the room.

In despair, as angry as the devil himself, I went to my room. I slept for a long time before my mother awakened me. Trembling, she urged me to run to my father's room. I shot down the corridor at the speed of light.

His breaths were slow but still audible. It was as though Abdulaziz were fighting for every breath of air. His chest rose as he strained to take in each atom of oxygen. Sitting by his side, I took his hand. I didn't know whether to clutch at my hair and roll on the floor, or continue to sit numbly beside my father. Those were terrifying and mysterious minutes. At times it felt as though the spirit had already left my father's body and right now he was gazing sternly down on me from above. Abdulaziz had always expected me to conduct myself with dignity and not show any pain or suffering. And so I went on sitting there like a statue.

They say that in the minute before death the person's entire life flashes before his eyes. At this moment, my father's life played before my eyes like a black and white film. The history of Abdulaziz was tragic but common enough in our era. It had been tragic from the moment he opened his eyes onto this sinful world. At the end of the 1930s, when this little Highlander was born, Soviet power had already deprived us of everything it could lay its hand on. Pastures, hundreds of heads of cattle, and two mills which had been the main providers of bread for the village. In the 1920s Bolshevik units arrived in the village and dozens of my kinsmen took to the mountains with their weapons. After ten years of brutal fighting my relatives were granted an amnesty in return for handing all their possessions over to the State. But by 1938, the year of the so-called Great Repression by Stalin, my grandfather, Ramzan, was arrested for being the son of a kulak. His young and pregnant wife was left without a husband a month after their wedding. Ramzan received ten years' hard labour and was sent to Siberia, to one of the thousands of camps in the Gulag system.

From there, in the summer of 1941, he was sent to fight in the Second World War. There was a the lack of fighting men to oppose the rapid German advance towards Moscow, so Stalin ordered anyone who was capable of holding a gun to join up. In 1942, in a place called Kerch in the Crimea, Ramzan was taken prisoner along with tens of thousands of other Soviet troops. Nothing has been heard of him since. And so the little Abdulaziz was left without a father in the third year of his life. In the winter of 1944 he and my grandmother were loaded into a cattle wagon with other Caucasian peoples, and sent to the Kazakh Steppe. That year, German forces pushed towards Baku with its vast oil reserves. Our mountains lay on their path. Joseph Stalin decided that we showed insufficient loyalty towards Communist power and therefore should be deported. On the three week journey to Kazakhstan they fed the passengers twice. Many people failed to reach their destination alive ...

... I sensed that my mother had crept into the room. She was sitting down by the wall and was softly weeping, a handkerchief pressed to her mouth. My father's breathing quickened. I went on holding his fading hand, but he was unaware of my touch.

My thoughts turned again to my grandmother. She and Abdulaziz were brought to a place called Golden Steppe on the border with China. They were left on the bare steppe land. There was nowhere for them to live or work. They dug pits with their bare hands, covering them with whatever they could lay their hands on, and there they slept. And this was the steppe where winters were so cold that the ground froze as hard as concrete. When spring arrived my grandmother was sent out to work on a collective farm, reaping millet. My father said that millet was their principal diet and because he ate it so often his teeth became covered in a yellow film, like glue. His mother would spend a long time scraping it off with a knife.

Towards the end of the war, in the summer of 1945, my grandmother succumbed to the intolerable living conditions. She developed pneumonia and died. My father was orphaned at the age of six. He was taken in by distant relatives of his mother, who had been sent to Siberia. After the death of the "father of the people" in 1953, Abdulaziz returned home to the Caucasus full of hatred for Soviet power and its false ideology. When he was eighteen he was called up to do his military service. At the end of his three year term he ended up in Kazakhstan, in the place where his mother was buried.

Bribing a local official, he found out the number of his mother's grave. At that time on the steppe, people were buried without formality. The corpse was simply flung into a pit and a plaque with a number placed above it. But owing to the severe climate of the region the numbers became indecipherable in a few years, or the plaque simply disappeared. And so, under cover of night, he began to dig up the graves. The severe frost made the earth so hard it was almost impossible to dig, even with a sledge hammer. In the first grave he found a man's bones. In the second, assorted remains. In the third, a young child. He worked for the next night, and the next, digging up seven or eight graves at a time. Towards dawn on the third night he found his mother's grave. He recognised her by her woollen socks. It was hard for me to imagine how a person must feel when he is on the Kazakh steppe in winter and comes upon the remains of his mother, the woman who gave him life, who suckled him, who spent countless sleepless nights by his bedside when he was teething or suffering from fever. As a son, he could not repay her in the way every son should. Perhaps this was why he went out there to gather her remains, to repay a debt which in normal life he would have repaid by other means.

Gathering her bones into a sheet, he carried them across the entire country so that he could bury her in her native mountains. The mullah recited a prayer, and her remains were re-buried in the village cemetery. Then he went to Siberia, where he worked as a labourer on a building site. At that time they were finding immeasurable reserves of oil and gas in Siberia. In order to extract these, it was necessary to construct living quarters for the oil workers, and so dormitories, roads and airports were built. My father said that life in Siberia was gruelling. Winter temperatures fell to minus forty-five degrees and in summer clouds of mosquitoes attacked the builders, making life unbearable. And the most terrible torment were the midges. They would land unnoticed on your head or an exposed area of skin and bite you. The pain was intolerable.

After a couple of years he applied to enter law school in the nearest city, Sverdlovsk, but because he persistently refused to join the Communist party, he was refused each time. Finally, at the age of 34, my father returned to his village the same simple man that he had been when he left after burying his mother's remains. Siberia had given Abdulaziz the benefit of meeting other Soviet peoples; it was there that he had developed as a human being. He had become acquainted with the harsh life of those parts and there he had formed his view of the Russians. He liked to repeat, - I was a hard drinker in Siberia for many years, but no-one ever laid a finger on me when I committed some sort of drunken stupidity. I think he had formed a very positive opinion of Russians and therefore did not want to go to war with them.

Returning to the village penniless, he married my mother and a year later I appeared. After I was born he returned to Siberia for a couple more years, in order to earn enough money to support Ayna and me.

In our parts it's unusual to have just one child. Five or six is the norm. Probably my father's health had something to do with it. He couldn't have any more. But my birth gave a new meaning to his existence. Sometimes I thought that he had returned to his native land in order to give me what he had never had himself - parental care, a direction in life, and help with education.

Towards the end of the 1970s he became attracted to Islam. In the USSR Islam and religion in general were blamed for many ills. As a man who was naturally anti-Soviet, Abdulaziz was interested in why Communism was so fearful of religion. What does this institution, which Marx called the opium of the people, have within it that makes the Communists try to suppress it so forcefully? Teaching himself Arabic through a dictionary, he began to make a detailed study of the history of the Islamic world, the Quran, the authenticity of the Hadiths, and the literature of those times. Therefore, it had been impossible for Doku and his Myrmidons to turn him into a zombie as they had done with other villagers.

– The more you know and the more arguments you can muster, the less others can wrap you around their little finger. Therefore I want you to study and be able to look more deeply at life than I was able to, - he said to me when

I began to prepare for my exams to enter college in Moscow. But I had no understanding then of what he was driving at.

A thin ray of light appeared above our heads. It gradually expanded, illuminating the room. I raised my head. At the end of a tunnel, I saw Azrael, the angel of death who appears before souls at the last moment of their lives. He was all in black; only his eyes blazed with fire. Around him cavorted little devils with forks in their hands. They grabbed my father's arm and tried to pull him upwards. He beat them off with his withered arm, and kicked them when they clutched his legs. Even in the last seconds of his life my father was not prepared to give up without a fight. My eyes were glued to the battle. But their strength was unequal - the devils went on pulling Abdulaziz towards the darkness. In an instant the picture vanished. I looked down and saw the lifeless body of my father. Abdulaziz had a beatific smile on his face. The grimaces of suffering that had scarred his face during the long months of his illness were wiped away. Even his cheeks had a slight flush.

"He no longer suffers; he is in paradise," I said to myself.

CHAPTER THIRTY THREE

The Funeral

Relatives came to open the gates of our house, letting everyone know of the loss that had befallen us. I don't remember exactly when, but after some time a mullah appeared. He sat down next to me. The room began to fill with people, mostly local aksakkals who had come to pay their final respects. The mullah whispered something in my ear, but I couldn't make out what the hell he was saying.

- Zaur, go along and get dressed. The room is full of people and you're sitting naked by the body of your father.

It was true, I was dressed only in the underpants I had been wearing when my mother called me to my father's room. Ayna went to get the living room ready for zikr, where the mullah would read verses from the Quran. An hour later they laid my father's body on a carpet and carried him through the garden behind the house. A relative wanted to start the ablutions ritual, but I said I would wash my father myself. The relative objected, saying that this was not customary, you had to follow the ritual and it should be accompanied by the reading of prayers. But I stood firm. Finally they decided I should wash my father in the presence of a relative. He would read a prayer and oversee that my action complied with Shariah law.

The effects of the cancer became clear to me as I began to wash my father for the second time in the past few days. There were no more than forty kilograms left of a formerly strong and healthy man. His right arm was as thin as a dried twig. The rest of his body was covered in yellow marks. A scar from the operation on his right shoulder, and a wound on his pelvis from which pus oozed - this was all that remained of Abdulaziz.

I began to wash my father's body. I wiped his legs. The relative recited the prayer. If once the Quranic verses had held me spellbound, now the sound of Arabic put me in a bad mood. Tears filled my eyes. When I reached my father's arm I lost control altogether, and began to kiss his hand. My relative paused in his recitation and tried to bring me to my senses, but I clung on to my father's hand and covered it in kisses. Tears ran from my eyes and mingled with the warm water. A lump rose in my throat and I wanted to burst into loud sobs. Only when I saw the thin wedding ring on my father's withered finger did I recover my senses a little. It had been my grandfather's wedding ring, given to him by my grandmother. My father wore it as a family memento.

Taking off the ring, I slipped it over my finger and began to feel more in control of myself. Wiping my tears, I left the garden and went to the living room where they were preparing to read from the Quran in honour of my father. I saw Doku among the guests, engaged in an animated discussion with the mullah. - Doku says we shouldn't read the fatikhe when we reach the end of the ceremony and perform zikr. He says it is not in Shariah law - the mullah came over to me and complained.

– Do what is customary for us - I replied.

It was all the same to me what we read at the end of the ceremony. At a time of great loss for our family how could anyone deliver a moral lecture on the correct way to bury the departed? Ever since I was a child I have known that at funerals we read the Quran and perform zikr, and the mullah ends the solemn rites with the first surah of the holy book, which is called fatikhe. In translation from Arabic, this means "opening the book". I really didn't want to become involved in this petty dispute, but the fact that Doku was trying to promote his ideology at the most inappropriate time wounded me. The mullah returned to his place. At the end of the proceedings he recited,

– Bismillah, ar-Rakhman, ar-Rakhim, Al'khamdulilya rabil' alyamin, the merciful, the gracious King on the day of judgement, we bow to you and ask for your aid. Lead us on a straight path, along the path that is blessed by you and not along ways that will arouse your wrath. May we never stray.

– Fatikhe - we responded, and passed our right hands over our faces. Doku did not follow suit.

At three o'clock in the afternoon the entire company set off for the village cemetery. A grave had already been dug. The children of the deceased usually bear the pall from the back, but I took a position at the front. Something prompted me to do everything in reverse today. People came out onto the street to see my father off on his last journey. Past the old shops and by the high school they took their turn in bearing the pall. Only as we walked in the shadow of the mosque walls did I slow down. We believe that the gates of heaven lie in the shadow of the mosque.

Abdulaziz's last resting place would be in the cemetery, alongside two fresh graves with tall poles stuck in them. In those graves lay young shaheeds[20]. As we were about to lay my father's body in his grave, Doku started up again.

– We have to lay the corpse on its back, - he announced.

– We have always buried the dead so that they lie on their right shoulders, and that is what we shall do, - Uncle Umar couldn't restrain himself. - If you, Long Beard, open your mouth one more time, I'll beat you like a dog. One glance at Uncle Umar assured me of the seriousness of his intentions.

– We'll follow our custom, Doku, - I said in a conciliatory tone. - Go on, you will be the imam during Namaz.

We usually performed Namaz right in the cemetery after a burial. My proposal delighted Doku, and he readily agreed. But I soon regretted having entrusted

---

20 Shaheed – martyr, one who has died fighting for their faith

the prayer reading to him. As he stood at the head of the group and bowed down for the first rakat, Umar crept up behind him and gave him a kick up the backside. He kicked with such force that the newly ordained imam went flying head first into a stream. It was just as well that Doku protected his face with his arm, or he would have broken his nose.

Everyone began to laugh at Umar's poor victim but no-one, not even Doku, retaliated, even though it is forbidden in our religion to touch someone while they are praying. Doku left the graveyard muttering something under his breath. When the time came for everyone to go back, I remained by the graveside.

"Goodbye, father, goodbye you good and honest man," I said to myself as I threw the last clod of earth onto his grave. "All that time when you were ill and almost never slept, no-one ever heard you moan or complain of your cruel end. You bore it all with great fortitude and you died like a true Highlander. For one also has to know how to die." For some reason, at that moment I recalled Dostoyevsky's words, - Why do you need an idol when you have the example of your father before you?

CHAPTER THIRTY FOUR

Ruslan return

Our family had not yet completed its year of mourning when Chechen fighters drove the Russians out of Grozny. The operation to recapture the capital bore no comparison, either in terms of its execution or on the level of its military cunning. An encirclement of the capital by fifty thousand fighters took the Russians by surprise. One group entered the city through the villages of Chechen Aul and Berdykel. Crossing height number 29, they stormed the large military base on the left side of the highway. It was the same one where I had found myself in 1995. After they had taken Grozny the Russians had also put it to use.

The second group, which entered from the town of Argun, demonstrated inspired cunning. Posing as a wedding party, a large convoy of cars filled with fighters and weapons pretended they were going to collect a bride in Grozny. All along the route they fired into the air and raised a hullabaloo. They showered the soldiers and officers at every checkpoint they passed with money, as though they were a real wedding procession. The Russians fell into the trap and the fighters entered the city without any problems. They said that one column of Russians, taken by surprise, could find nothing better to do than to take hostage local Chechen police, who had been on their side. They tied them to armoured cars, and flying white flags, they left the city in the direction of Khankali.

Twenty-five days later, on the thirty-first of August, a peace accord was signed in Khasov Yurt, and the withdrawal of federal troops from the republic began. On that day we had a real celebration in our village. It had been a long time since I had seen such happy people, who were finally able to express their joy and relief. Almost everyone in the village came out onto the streets, and singing and dancing began. Uncle Zalimkhan brought out his old accordion and a dance floor was improvised near the mosque. I was the only one who didn't dance that day. There was no-one to dance with. Ruslan and Emi were far away and I wasn't used to dancing with anyone else, nor did I feel inclined to. But that didn't spoil my mood. It was one of the happiest days of my life.

The next three years passed almost unnoticed. I couldn't make up my mind what to do. I even stopped reading Nizami's book about Alexander. I did not feel the need. Once, I had wanted to study and get a higher education, but that no longer attracted me. To get married and start a family attracted me even less. For whole days at a time I sat in my father's room and read through his books. These works taught me one thing: that knowledge, education and intellect are important, but not of the greatest importance. The most important thing in life is harmony. When academic knowledge, God-given instincts, persistence, initiative, physical strength and - if you like - looks, ability to relate to others, charisma, and a thousand other smaller qualities combine harmoniously in one individual, it will be that individual that makes history. I didn't have to look far to find an example. Ruslan belonged to that category of human beings.

It was no accident that I was thinking of my friend. A few days ago he had returned to the village after an absence of four years. During that time he had become the person he was destined to become – a leader of distinction. His qualities were needed in time of war. From the moment that he had given me a gun in Shtoum Kale and then returned to Grozny, he had fought in the fiercest battles, including in Grozny and Shalin. In one of those battles he was wounded and taken to Turkey for an operation. In 1997 he was elected to be a parliamentary deputy, and he was still carrying out undercover operations against the federal forces in our district.

At first I regretted that I had gone to meet him. In his newly-renovated house there was not enough room to swing a cat. Members of his *teyp*, neighbours and guests from the surrounding area, and still more people whom no-one even knew, turned up to greet him. Each one had their request: for work, to settle an argument with an enemy *teyp*, and many more. On the other hand, I hadn't seen him for a long time. In the last four years he had only called once to offer his condolences over my father's death.

Ruslan had changed a lot, both in character and appearance. He had matured a great deal during those years. His eyes still blazed with passion but his behaviour had changed enormously. He listened to people very attentively and never offered his opinion straightaway, but would make his decision only after gathering information from his own sources. His mind had become very analytical and enquiring so that it was now almost impossible to deceive or manipulate him.

At around eleven in the evening, having spoken to all the guests, he and I were left alone in the room. He looked tired so I didn't want to detain him for long.

–   You know that Washington is ugly, - he said to me suddenly.

–   Well, I saw him in a photo. He seemed to be an old man with a big nose, - I said in surprise.

–   Oh, you're the same simpleton you always were, - he burst out laughing. - I meant the city of Washington.

–   Well, you tell me, how would I know what Washington was like? I would hardly be able to find it on a map.

Ruslan went on to tell me that Washington is a large gloomy city where everyone wears suits and masses of black people hang around the streets begging for cigarettes or a couple of dollars, and there is a slum right behind the White House. At first I thought that his friends in Grozny had told him all this rubbish but, no, he brought out his passport and showed me an American visa.

–   I was a member of the delegation that visited Washington last year with President Maskhadov. They greeted us like heroes, especially in the Senate, where there were a couple of senators who had fought against the Russians in Afghanistan, - said Ruslan briefly.

'Amazing,' I said to myself. 'Ruslan has been to America, has been in the white marble House of Congress, in the State Department, and in their centres for political analysis, and after all that he is still complaining about it. For the vast majority of Chechens, or rather the absolute majority, the chance of going to America was as distant as that of flying to Mars.

—   And is that all you have to say about America? - I moaned. - What about McDonalds, Levi jeans, expensive cars and wide streets?

—   Only poor people eat in McDonalds: blacks; Mexicans; Ethiopians. The wealthy eat in the nice areas of Georgetown, which is in the centre of Washington. All in all, it is dull there, and humid, especially in August which is when we went. And basically they shat on us. A couple of old boys in the Senate loved us but that was only because they had fought against the Russians themselves. It is a city where only one thing has any value, and that is money.

—   But that's not important, - he continued, - in the State Department, President Maskhadov gave a speech which moved all those present. He said that many leaders come here to talk about independence, sovereignty, democracy, and many other such things, but we are one of the few peoples who have shown, through the shedding of blood, that we deserve independence. Some of the Americans even shed tears on hearing these words, or perhaps they were just pretending to cry. Hypocrisy is also a trait of these people, - said Ruslan.

I was in shock. Could it really be that bad? How could they not care about our suffering, our war, which cost the lives of five lads from my class alone? How could it have turned out like this? Where is the justice? For America itslf was founded as a result of war against Great Britain. More than anyone, the Americans should have been able to understand us.

Ruslan had a different opinion. - I tell you again, their main aim is to weaken Russia, and how and with whom, and how many people die in the process, whether they are Chechens, Tartars, Bashkirs, Yakuts, they don't give a shit. Politics is pitiless and also without principle or conscience, - he said to me.

Something inside me rebelled against Ruslan's words. I don't know why but, for me, America meant the promised land, like in the Bible. Nothing could shake that faith. A land of endless opportunities. Perhaps Ruslan or President Maskhadov had had too many unrealistic expectations of the kind of help the USA might give in our fight against the Russians, and when those hopes failed to bear fruit, they began to criticise America, I don't know ...

Whatever the case, the fact remained that for me, a lad from the mountains, America remained a stronghold of order and justice. Then Ruslan told me that there had been a serious split in our government that day. The concept of Chechen independence had entered its second stage. Now the religious radicals and former war heroes were scrambling for lucrative positions in government. Shirvani, the brother of Shamil Basaev, had been made Minister of Oil Production. Basaev himself and Movladi Udugov had allied with the radicals. In Gudermes, Urus Martan and on Minutka Square in Grozny, there were real battles taking place with the Wahhabis.

– I can't understand how it's come to this. We fought, we were prepared to give what was most holy to us, our lives, for an independent Chechnya. And so everyone rose as one, took up arms and went to fight. But now we can't even reach agreement on the simplest questions. How have we fallen so far, from lofty ideas to base and petty intrigue and political infighting? - Ruslan asked.

It seemed to me that he simply wanted to pour out his heart, and to whom better than me, his childhood friend, who had not yet been corrupted by life, and in whom he could trust? It was long after midnight. Ruslan went on talking about the political troubles in Grozny. Even I felt tired. Finally he said that the radicals had formed a powerful coalition and in a few days there would be an important announcement from the capital. On that disturbing note, we parted. In any case, tomorrow there would be a wedding in the village, between Al Rashid and one of Doku's relatives. We would continue our discussion there. Ruslan still had a lot to tell me.

CHAPTER THIRTY FIVE

Shaitan's wedding

It was a terrible day for me in every sense. The wedding of the Arab, Al Rashid, who had already caused trouble among us, had become an important occasion. During the war, the Arab had distinguished himself in fighting against the Russians and acquired some political importance. His marriage to a Chechen girl would strengthen his position still further, and make him popular among the ranks of Chechens.

I deliberately turned up late to the house where the wedding was taking place. I don't like spending a long time at weddings, and especially not at this one. I was only going there to show my face, or as we say, to put a 'tick' against my name. I only had to turn up and slip away after a couple of hours. In the room, so-called Communism reigned again. The young people sat with the aksakkals on the carpet-covered floor. A speech played on the tape recorder; it was an Arabic nashid. It reminded me more of a funeral than a wedding. No merry-making, no heart to heart discussions or toasts brimming with emotion, no music and no dancing. The women were nowhere to be seen. In our weddings they bring in the food and make some wisecracks, and the young people dance until they drop.

I went in and greeted everyone with a nod of my head. Ruslan was sitting in the middle of the floor; there were a lot of people around him. Al Rashid and some other Arabs sat in the places of honour. Ruslan called me over, indicating an empty place by his side.

—   I saved this place for you, - he said. It was a nice gesture on his part.

—   But the most important news is this, - he continued in a half whisper. - The Arab's bride is only fourteen years old.

—   Who told you?

— Have you just fallen from the moon? Don't you know what goes on in this small village of yours?

— And her parents agreed? - I turned to him in distress. It didn't seem right to me that a girl of that age should be given in marriage. She was still a child. It's true that before the revolution we married young, but with the arrival of the Bolsheviks all that business was quietly forgotten. And now, after almost a hundred years, we were again going back to medieval customs.

Suddenly Al Rashid and a quartet of his fellow tribesmen slipped out of the room and went into the adjoining one. I could not understand why.

— Doku told the girl's parents that, in accordance with the words of the prophet, a girl could marry very young, - my friend went on in an ironic tone. - If she can withstand the blow of a broom and not fall down it means she is ripe for marriage. And so they gave her to Al Rashid. So now you see what we have come to.

— It makes me wonder why we endured so much, why so many of us died, just to reach this state, - I agreed.

— Mark my words, when the next war with the Russians begins, and it will, no-one from the highlands will go. Everyone's sick of all this turmoil and intrigue, thefts, kidnapping, and such like shit.

— Look, - he said, glancing towards the places vacated by the guests. - what kind of democracy we have. I no longer know which is better, our so-called democracy or the Russian occupation, which didn't have all these disgraceful practices.

There was nothing more to say. In a couple of minutes, the Arabs returned. They were chatting about something and gesticulating. Their agitation certainly had nothing to do with the wedding. Having sat for half an hour or so, and having had something to eat, we were preparing to leave when I heard a disturbance in the street. It was already dark so I couldn't see who was fighting or, more importantly, what it was about. But a crowd had gathered. The young people poured out of the room into the street.

– What are they fighting about? - I asked.

– Words were exchanged and two groups of youths started to fight. They are young and hot-headed, and what's more they are armed, - one of my acquaintances replied. - It seems that nothing much actually happened. Two young guys were arguing over who should go first down the street. Neither wanted to let the other pass. They began to fight, an aksakkal stepped in and the matter was soon sorted out.

Just then, Ruslan gave me a nudge and signalled to me to follow him out of the room. Carefully, glancing behind him as though he feared we might be followed, he led me down the street. A hundred metres further on we saw a man standing in the shadows. Ruslan beckoned him over.

– He's one of my guys; he speaks Arabic like a native, - he told me.

It was the first time I had seen this man, who was a bit older than me and had red hair.

– Well, tell me, what were they doing there, going back and forth?

Ginger didn't want to speak in front of me but his boss insisted, saying I could be trusted.

– What a bright guy that Al Rashid is. He's a real genius, - said the agent sarcastically. Five minutes before the news is shown on NTV, he and his companions come into the room to watch it. But nothing except Yeltsin interests him.

180

– You see what true followers of Islam we have among us. They forbid ordinary people to watch TV as it is the instrument of Satan, but they can't take their eyes off it themselves, - said my friend.

– But the most interesting thing is, boss, - Ginger went on. - Al Rashid says that Yeltsin is going to resign soon.

– What? Did they announce it on TV? - I asked doubtfully.

– No, he simply said that for three days in a row, NTV had not shown a close-up of Yeltsin. Only from a distance and very briefly. Last time that happened was in 1996, just before they operated on him. After watching this, the Arab spoke to some other Arab on the phone and said there would soon be a significant change taking place in the Kremlin. Al Rashid said to his guy that Yeltsin's days are numbered, - the red-haired man concluded.

– Are you sure you heard correctly? - Ruslan pressed him. The agent nodded. Ruslan thanked him for the information and told him he could go and rest.

It seems that security had had the Arab under surveillance for a long time. All his movements, his meetings and his phone conversations had been monitored. Aslan Maskhadov and Vice President Vakha Arsanov knew that our foreign guest was playing his games here. And that in the space of a few days he might turn everything upside down. Therefore they kept him under close surveillance.

– Late at night, when everyone was asleep, the man I call Ginger entered the house where the wedding was to take place. Unnoticed, he made some tiny holes in the ceiling of the room, so that he could see and hear what was going on. As silently as a cat, he crept barefoot over the roof in order to find out what the Arab was doing. We even arranged a fight in the street so that Ginger could slip away and hide while everyone was distracted by the noise, - Ruslan explained.

Unfortunately, by the end of the day our small victory was overshadowed by another event. On the third of February 1999, President Maskhadov, under the influence of extremists, announced that Sharia law would be fully implemented, which meant a change from our secular organs of power to religious bodies. Before this, some elements of Sharia law had entered our legal procedures. A year before our President's official announcement a couple had been shot dead in Grozny for living together outside of marriage. But now the official adoption of Sharia law had deprived Ichkeria of the moral support of the global community.

The next morning, Ruslan came to excuse himself. He was going back to Grozny. An emergency session of parliament had been called.

– We are taking a very wrong course, - said my friend the deputy, as he left. - Before this, we were seen as a country who stood up to Russia, who fought for freedom, as Czechoslovakia, Hungary, Poland and the Baltic countries did in their time. It was our ticket to joining the civilised world. Now what? Who in the west is going to publicly support a country that is like Iran or Somalia?

Having said this, he looked at me intently as though he wanted to say something more important. I know Ruslan through and through, so I asked him straight out what he meant by that meaningful look.

– I was wondering whether to tell you or not ... Forget about that trouble in Grozny for a minute. To hell with it. I have to tell you something important. I'm afraid I might not get a second chance like this.

– Well, don't stand on ceremony, spit it out! - I said rather coarsely. I couldn't stand this dithering.

– My agent Ginger heard the Arabs mentioning your father yesterday. Seeing us together at the wedding, Al Rashid said to his companion, - It's a good thing his father is dead. Otherwise he would have ruined this wedding with his speeches.

For a minute I failed to grasp what my friend had just told me. But when it sunk in, I calmly asked for more information. I could tell from his face that Ruslan was surprised that I wasn't shouting or tearing my hair. At moments of crisis, self-control was my closest ally. 'Right, so this means there was no accidental fall, he was attacked and he fell as a result', I thought to myself.

Immediately I began to make a plan of action. Ruslan guessed my thoughts.

–   Look, don't do anything stupid, - he said. - Ginger's report doesn't prove anything, but it evokes serious suspicions. We need to gather more information, and as soon as we have incontrovertible evidence we deliver a swift and mortal blow. if you take revenge you can count on me.

With these words, he got into his car.

I was plunged into dark thoughts about the Arab and unable even to bid Ruslan a proper farewell.

I was not to know then that it would be our last meeting.

CHAPTER THIRTY SIX

Training Camp

Towards the middle of March, it became clear to us in the village that we were heading towards war again. Al Rashid returned to the village with his pregnant wife and Doku called everyone together in the central square. Al Rashid behaved as though he had lived here all his life. He greeted the villagers like family, embracing some and exchanging warm words with them. Doku opened the meeting by saying that, according to the information he had, a second war would begin soon. Forces were gathering once more on the border with Dagestan and the Stavropol region. He said this would be our last war with the Russians.

— Five years ago we were taken unawares. We had nothing, neither weapons nor military skills, nor support from our Muslim brothers. - At that moment our eyes turned involuntarily to the Arab. - But by the grace of Allah we were able to bring the mighty Russia to her knees, and we will do it again. Allahu akbar!

A cry of Allahu akbar rang out, and the crowd grew excited. Doku had set the right tone for the gathering. The next person to speak was Al Rashid but, after listening to him for several minutes, the villagers' enthusiasm diminished. Shaitan spoke the truth. He presented his arguments logically, but all the same he struck a wrong note. 'It would be better if you hadn't spoken,' I said to myself.

— A long time ago, the Russian swine came here to kill us, but they failed, - he said in broken Russian. - And now they can't do anything, we won't let them. Six kilometres from here in the depths of a gorge, we are preparing a camp for training warriors. Your brothers from many countries will be there; Arabs, Turks, Daghestanis, Uighurs, Uzbeks. We are preparing for jihad. You must also come if you don't want the Russians to catch us unawares.

— Allahu akbar! - shouted Doku and several villagers.

It was the chance I had been waiting for. I had to go to the training camp, watch him, and discover whether the Arab had been involved in my father's death, and if so, how. I had a good chance of clarifying all this in the camp. I was counting on being able to overhear a casual conversation, as Ginger had done at Al Rashid's wedding, for example, or perhaps I would find some other proof of involvement.

I didn't know for sure... but then Alexander, going into battle with the Russians' horned monster, didn't know how the fight would end. Only by going in to fight himself, face to face, one on one, was he able to see his enemy's weak spot. I too could find an answer to the question that troubled me by staying close to the Arab and observing him.

Al Rashid's unblinking eyes shone. Together with some lads of eighteen or nineteen who had survived the first war, I signed up to train to fight. However the majority of villagers, especially former fighters, did not exactly burn with desire. No-one wanted to climb up into the mountains again. They gave us a day to get ready. The next morning we gathered at the same place and they held a roll call. The majority of the old guard failed to turn up. They were battle-hardened soldiers and didn't need any extra training. At the roll call they counted off twenty-two people. Of these, three were experienced soldiers who bore arms.

After call-up we set off for the camp. I was familiar with the first part of our route, which followed the course of the River Chanti Argun, one of the tributaries of the Argun, flowing towards the Pankisi Gorge. But after a couple of hours we made a sharp turn and plunged into the depths of the forest. There was no clear path, it was virgin forest, and so we progressed very slowly. First, we had to keep ascending and descending, and second, the wet earth clung to our boots. In fact, our boots became heavier and heavier; every half hour we stopped, scraping off the mud before continuing.

Climbing another five ridges, we reached a small clearing at the foot of a hill. The camp was laid out around this hill. There were trenches dug into the ground designed as underground barracks in which we would sleep, but as yet they had no coverings. We were deathly tired after hours of walking and so no-one complained about the camp not being ready. I sat straight down on the muddy ground and rested my back against a huge tree. After ten minutes I started to feel cold. You only have to lie down for a couple of minutes for the mountains to remind you of their harsh nature. I went to sit by the fire; they gave me a can of stew which I heated up and ate.

– It's going to be a bit uncomfortable today, but we'll get up early and arrange everything, - said Doku, handing me a hunk of bread. - We'll divide into two groups and build our training installations. We'll cover the dug-outs with logs and line the inside walls with them. Tomorrow, Al Rashid will come with more fighters and instructors.

– Will we begin to train soon? - someone asked.

– I don't know, but the technical business of training usually takes a month. The most important thing is to show you how things work and make sure you have mastered everything. A single mistake in battle means death. The faster you learn, the faster we will finish the training.

It was growing dark and we circled the fire like shamans. No-one wanted to withdraw from it. It grew very cold, below freezing. We threw more wood onto the fire but we just could not get warm. About one in the morning, we decided to lie down. We left one guy to keep the fire burning but still we could not fall asleep. A sudden noise, like children crying, started up. Those lads who were not local but who had grown up in towns immediately sprung up on their guard. They probably thought that they were starting to hallucinate. The reality was less mysterious. A pack of jackals was circling around us. When they howl, it sounds like small children crying. Although I had heard their howls since childhood, I still hated them. 'To hell with these mountains, as soon as I find out something I'll go and join Ruslan,' I said to myself. I still couldn't fall asleep. My whole body shivered with cold and my teeth chattered. It was the longest night of my life.

When morning came, everyone was frozen stiff. We huddled together around the fire, eager to drink hot tea. Opening my holdall, I pulled out my toothbrush and paste. It had been a habit of mine since childhood to clean my teeth in the morning. A few lads looked askance at me, but this was not a question of hygiene.

– Where can I get water? - I asked.

– You have to go that way for two or three minutes. There's a stream, - but Doku spoke loudly so that everyone could hear. - No-one is to pee there, or perform other necessities, closer than a hundred metres from the spot where we fetch water.

– Do you take us for animals? Never speak to us about such matters again, - one of my fellow villagers flared up.

– This is not a health spa, nor is it a restaurant, nor a kindergarten. Everyone has to understand why we're here, and not show weakness, - Doku shouted, even more harshly.

After the first night in the camp everyone's nerves were on edge. It was a good job the mullah hadn't quarrelled with one of the experienced soldiers, as they had brought their automatic weapons with them. Who knows what might have happened then? For myself, I decided that our half-built camp was like Chicago of the 1930's and I would have to watch my tongue. Deciding not to tempt fate, I went down to fetch water. It was so cold that my teeth began to chatter again and my fingers turned as red as prawns. In any case, I had no other choice. Collecting some water, I returned to the camp. Relative calm had descended. Having drunk our tea, everyone warmed up and relaxed a bit. We should have begun to build up the camp, but Doku sat quietly and we followed suit, sitting until two in the afternoon, when Al Rashid's unit arrived with around thirty new recruits.

Only then did the camp really spring to life. We chopped down trees and sawed them into logs. With these we lined the insides and created the roofs of the dugouts. I worked harder than anyone. I wanted to show my determination to fight the Russians. I had to lull the suspicions of my enemy who was as sly as a fox. In a word, I laboured with all my strength. We had a centuries-old tradition, where the village organised a work-day to build a house for newlyweds, a mosque, a bridge or some other necessary infrastructure, and it came into play here. And so the day passed in a blink of an eye. As night fell we were still building a roof over our temporary dwelling place.

—   No-one will shiver tonight, - the Arab tried to cheer us up. - There are a lot of us here and there won't be enough room for everyone in our barracks. But in the morning we'll make two more spacious barracks so there'll be enough for everyone for a hundred years.

Having said this, Al Rashid burst out laughing. His laughter gave us the creeps. Were we going to spend the next hundred years in battle?

—   Take off your boots and lay them beneath your head like a pillow, - said an unknown man to me as we crawled into our barracks to sleep.

—   Why? - I asked with curiosity.

—   Al Rashid told us to. He said that way our boots would dry out and it would be comfortable for our heads.

The eyes of the unknown lad shone with unshakeable faith in the Arab's words.

– Well let's try it, - I answered, wiping all the mud off a boot, I laid it beneath my head. It was uncomfortable and awkward, but as we had been working for the whole day I fell asleep quickly.

When I woke in the morning, I found that what my companion had said was true. My head was intact and my boots were dry. My new acquaintance was called Faizul. He came from a suburb of Argun. His father had died during the Russians' cleansing campaign. They did not kill him directly, but when they took his eldest son from the house, his elderly heart could not stand it and he died from a massive heart attack. It was the desire to avenge his father and elder brother, whom the family later ransomed from a torture chamber, that brought Faizul to the camp.

Faizul was a light-haired village lad of medium height. A typical highlander, he was honest, straightforward and completely lacking in guile. I would even have said simple. For example, he thought Darwin was a first name and he had heard something about the discovery of Copernicus but he didn't believe in that theory. This didn't prevent me from befriending him. First, who the hell needs Darwin and Copernicus in the mountains? Second, he had something that is lacking in many cultured and educated sons of 'good families'. And that is trustworthiness. Trustworthiness is one of the few things that money can't buy. You can't acquire it through patronage or inherit it. It's like being pregnant, you either are or you aren't. And for that reason I latched on to Faizul.

The next morning they divided us into two groups. The first had to finish building the barracks, and the second had to prepare a training ground. Although it was a tough job, we finished constructing the underground dugout in one day, and then went to have a look at the training ground. It was in the form of an ellipse, with a wooden obstacle course around the perimeter that you had to climb or jump over. There was also a tunnel which you had to crawl through. I decided not to try that. 'Who will wash my clothes afterwards?' I asked myself.

At nine in the morning of our third day in the camp, they started training without giving us breakfast. The Arab asserted that you can't train on a full stomach. I thought they'd teach us about mines and the nuances of battle in forests, but it didn't happen. The Arab announced that we would start by running three to four kilometres. We had jogged for less than two hundred metres when rapid machine gun fire burst out close by. Some of us threw ourselves to the ground in fear; some simply scattered in all directions. 'It's the end, we've fallen into a Russian ambush,' was my first thought. Only Al Rashid remained cool, and he was very cool. All eyes were upon him.

— Why are you on the ground? Go on, run, run everybody! - he yelled. - Don't stop, run further, - Shaitan continued to shout.

Gradually recovering ourselves, we began to run again. But again machine gun fire rattled over our heads. The Arab repeated that we were not to be afraid but just run. After ten minutes we were racing as though scalded, bullets whistling to the side and over our heads. Thirty minutes after we had started to run, half the unit collapsed. They lay where they fell. Some were paralysed by fear, others breathless and exhausted. And some complained of the weight of their battle dress. I could barely move my legs, and I was desperately thirsty.

— So you see, it's not a holiday camp, - the Arab persisted. - That's what battle is like. You have to be able to hold yourself together, not lose your cool and keep together as a unit. For each of these points today, I give you a 'C'. Congratulations.

After these last words, he again burst into hearty laughter. His assistants emerged from the dense forest around us. It was they who had been shooting at us. And so during the course of the week we ran through the forest under fire and each time we reacted less. Many of us could even distinguish the fire of Kalashnikovs from Stechkin bullets. From the 'Kalashas' there was a powerful echo and they reminded you of a bee's flight. Stechkins sounded like the motor of a rackety old tractor.

We crawled, ran and jumped through all the obstacles around the camp, and then the time came when they announced that they would teach us how to handle explosives. I wanted to be a sniper and didn't understand why they were teaching me about mines. But the instructors insisted. They said that snipers had to set mines to the flanks and the rear so the enemy didn't catch us unawares. They promised to show us how to lay mines and explosives everywhere, from tree branches a little bit higher than an armoured car, so the Russians would be blown up, in vehicles left off the road, and also we were taught how to give them little surprises when the mine could be disguised as anything you like, such as a toy mouse, a bottle of cola, military supplies and many other things. The trouble was, I was mortally afraid of mines and anything that would blow up. I couldn't imagine how I would learn all subtleties of explosives. I was shaking inside.

CHAPTER THIRTY SEVEN

Invasion

While we were training in the camp, the Basaev and Khattab detachments had entered Daghestan. It was said that Basaev's forces had treacherously attacked a Daghestani village and because of that, the Russians invaded Chechnya for a second time. All this was untrue. Six months before Basaev's raid, the Russians had again begun to concentrate troops on the border with Ingushetia and several days before the Chechen incursion into Daghestan, Russian convoys had crossed the border into the Shelkovsky and Nadterechny districts in the south of the country. A small Russian unit had occupied the Argun Gorge, cutting off the means of escape into Georgia. We were preparing to attack one of these convoys.

We took our positions in the early morning. We had walked through the night, it was safer then, and most importantly it was cooler. It was now summer. We had great difficulty climbing up the far side of the gorge. For a long time Al Rashid sought a projection onto which he could tie his rope. Throwing my rope over a large tree stump, I began to climb. With his huge backside, the Arab was the slowest of all. Then we pulled up our rocket launchers. Al Rashid surveyed the road through his binoculars, and gave orders as to who was to stand where and how they were to camouflage themselves.

The inhabitants of the nearest village of Jari would give a sign when the convoy passed. It was my first military operation, and I was very nervous. Faizul on the other hand, sat calmly. He acted as though he had spent his whole life in a mercenary training camp and was a now professional fighter.

We fired down on the convoy without mercy. Most of the soldiers never even knew what had hit them.

— OK, that's it. I'm going down now, with Allah's help, - said Faizul, as Shaitan descended with another fighter. The Russians were putting up resistance on the road but Faizul didn't pay any attention. He ran towards the enemy, firing non-stop. It was sheer suicide. 'We have to give him cover,' I thought to myself. Confusion reigned on the road. After the petrol tanks of the URAL lorries started to explode, the remaining soldiers retreated towards the river. Two machine guns awaited them there, firing non-stop. Two of the soldiers tried to hide beneath the corpses of their fallen comrades, but Faizul threw a grenade towards them, and then pulled the pin of another and threw it after the first. After two explosions three seconds apart the business was finished.

We could hear the groans of the dying soldiers. In order to finish them off, Faizul let off another round of machine gun fire. When there were no more doubts, my friend approached the corpses, cut off an ear, wrapped it in a handkerchief and placed it in his pocket.

– That's it. We can go home now, - he said.

'I wish I shared your joy, Faizul,' I thought to myself. When would I be able to say the same? When would my agony be over? How long would I have to live with my doubts? There were moments when I just wanted to shoot the Arab and be done with it, to put an end to this nightmare.

The angry voice of Al Rashid pulled me back to reality. He was standing over the corpse of the officer who had just been shot, shouting something.

One of our fighters wanted to cut the stars from the officer's shoulder strap and this displeased our commander. Whether this was just for show or as a sign of genuine respect, was a mystery to me. It was ten in the evening by the time we reached the camp. Almost everyone collapsed from exhaustion.

– An hour's rest and then we get going, - Doku shouted.

His order alarmed us. After five hours on the march, my body ached all over. I didn't have the strength for yet another one. An hour later, when Doku called us together, most of the unit was still peacefully sleeping. He entered our barracks and ordered us all to get up. But no-one wanted to leave their place of warmth. Grumbling, he went back to the barracks and shouted for Al Rashid.

I awoke just before dawn. At first I was reluctant to get up and go down to the river to clean my teeth, thinking that this was our last day in that camp and I might as well use the time to get some more sleep. On the other hand, I knew that Doku and Al Rashid would soon rise for morning prayers, and as soon as they had finished they would order us all to get up. Then there would be a long trek to the next camp and I would curse myself if I hadn't cleaned my teeth. More than anything in the world I hated the sour taste of unbrushed teeth in my mouth.

The forest had not yet awoken. Only the babble of the stream and the morning song of birds broke the silence. With toothbrush in my mouth, I absorbed the beauty all around me.

The idyll was penetrated by a strange sound coming from far away. I wondered what it could be. A second later I was deafened by a metallic roar; another second and everything lit up. The ground rose towards me. Something hit my leg with terrible force; I even heard the sound of breaking bones. Then everything went black. 'This is the end,' I thought.

I awoke in agony. I was freezing cold, lying on the far bank of the stream covered in earth and large tree branches. I couldn't move, I seemed to be paralysed. I had not the strength to move my arms and free myself from everything that lay on top of me. And my leg – it did not just hurt, it made my whole body shake with pain. I howled in agony.

What could I do? 'Allah has left me to be eaten by jackals. And if not jackals, then I'll bleed to death.' I thought. I tried to muster all my strength. Like a computer, my mind began to calculate all possible means of escape. I suddenly remembered what the Arab had said, that if we were captured, the Russians would torture us. In order to bear the pain, we had to think of our families and loved ones killed in battle, and about the most terrible things we had endured in the war.

I remembered the little boy who had been shot through the leg on the outskirts of Grozny, and the young woman who held her baby to her breast to shelter it from the bullets. These pictures swam before my eyes and the sense of hatred did its work. I felt my strength return. I slowly reached out for a twig, brought it to my mouth and clenched it between my teeth. Each movement made the pain in my leg worse but I began to clear myself of all the soil that covered me. First I threw off the earth, then I freed myself from the remnants of trees that lay on me. The hardest thing was to free my leg; it was caught between two large river rocks in such a position that I could not push them away. It was too painful to raise myself, and even if I could have borne the pain, I did not have enough strength in my arms to move them.

I could hear groans coming from the camp. I couldn't imagine what had befallen them or what state they were in now. I looked around for a tree branch that would be strong enough. There was a suitable piece of wood to my side but it lay out of reach. Those nearby were very short and pointed at the ends, but there was no choice. I grabbed a bough and thrust it between the stone and my leg. Hideous pain shot through my whole body but I knew that if I stopped now it would be even worse. I pushed harder. When the branch went in deep enough, I began to twist it towards my leg. I clenched my teeth so hard that the twig in my mouth snapped. Spitting it out, I began to twist the wood. The rock shifted a tiny bit and then a bit more, until I finally managed to extract my leg.

What had happened to it? All I could see down there was a bloody mess. I reached the camp by hopping on one leg. Just beyond the second barracks was a huge rocket crater. It was surrounded by scorched trees, torn up by their roots. The barracks had also been torn apart, as though an excavator had scooped it up and hurled it back down again. All those who had been sleeping there were probably dead. All around were scattered pieces of weaponry, clothing and food.

I called out to Faizul. No sound came from beneath the logs, neither groans nor cries. There was a deathly silence. When I peered into the barracks, I saw someone's crushed back. I could only see the spine and a pool of blood around it. I couldn't see whose body it was. I went a little further to look at the other underground barracks. Just in case, I picked up a gun I found lying on the ground. Beside the Arab's quarters, among scattered belongings, I saw something so shocking and unexpected that my physical pain faded. Desperately, I began to hunt for the Arab. I had to find him, dead or alive.

CHAPTER THIRTY EIGHT

Alexander's Egyptian campaign

Alexander had conquered half the world, and still he continued his campaigns. Kanuje in Kyrgyzia, Kairouan in Tunisia, Serendib on the island of Ceylon, and Jerusalem in Palestine were the next cities to be seized by his forces. Before he decided to go back to his homeland of Rum, to rest, the great leader spent some time holding banquets and distributing the spoils of war to the soldiers and inhabitants of Macedonia.

One day he heard shouting from beyond the palace walls. It was Egyptians from the banks of the Nile who had come to petition him. They had been attacked by hitherto unknown tribes from central Africa.

– We are fighting with barbarians, the like of which have never been seen before in God's world,- said an Egyptian elder. - They launch surprise attacks in pitch darkness and they are led by forces of darkness; otherwise, how would they manage to catch us unawares? For they come in no small detachments, but in a huge army whose numbers know no bounds.

– What do your wise men say about this military cunning? - asked the ruler of Rum.

– They say the army hides in the sand and so they manage to reach the city unnoticed.

– Not in the sand, but in the waters of the Nile, - a second petitioner disagreed.

– They are winged demons, they invade from the air, - a third added.

The story intrigued Alexander. After listening to the petitioners, Aristotle's keen mind was perplexed but he knew one thing for certain, if he defeated this unknown army, it would mean that it was weaker than his own, and he would rightfully become the ruler of the world. He turned to Aristotle for advice.

Aristotle's reply was brief: - Your happiness is your defence and your right, crush the dragon with all your might.

A hasty call-up, and they were on their way. In a couple of months, Alexander's forces stood face to face with the Zanji. Both armies were so huge that wild animals fled before the sound of the iron-clad hooves of their horses. Alexander had a favourite, Tutianush, light-hearted and silver of tongue. It was said that he, like Alexander, could extract secrets from anyone, so the great leader decided to entrust Tutianush with a most important mission - to use his silver tongue to touch the heart of the leader of the Zanji, and persuade him to exchange prisoners.

Tutianush obeyed, and went over to the enemy camp. He spoke clearly and passionately. He described everything to the enemy - Alexander's military genius and the way he had conquered cities. - No-one has defeated Alexander in over thirty years and neither will you, - he added, - It will be too late, we'll ignite such slaughter, that all the seas won't quench the flames, so where will you find water?

The leader of the Zanji was not impressed by these words. He answered that they were beside the largest sea in the world and there was enough water for ten armies. The Zanji guards seized Tutianush and cut off his head. His blood was carried in a cup to the head of the tribe and he drank it in huge gulps, just as my uncle Umar had drunk the bull's blood during a Ramadan holiday. The news of Tutianush's fate drove Alexander into a rage. He turned as red as a burning reed, his foe had shamed him, Tutianush's fate shocked everyone. The next morning the commander forbade his troops to go into battle. He was sure that in such a state as they were in, they would lose. Again he called Aristotle to advise him.

- I want to retreat. This had to happen at some point, I can't go on winning victories for ever.

- Great One, we can't retreat, we are on the Nile Delta. From here you can reach any part of the world, or rather conquer any part of the world. If you retreat, you will lose all that you have gained.

- We can't give battle so it means we shall die here in order to be glorified by future generations, - Alexander revealed his thoughts.

- The Zanji are snakes. They have neither honour nor dignity. They are people without reason and so nothing holds them back from doing evil. Therefore they killed your emissary without a thought. In order to scare such people, we have to be more cruel, more bloodthirsty than they can imagine. I know how to strike terror into their hearts.

Aristotle advised him to send out scouts to capture several Zanji and bring them to Alexander's tent, and the ruler of Rum must appear before the enemy's prisoners, not as a human being but as an evil and bloodthirsty sorcerer. Then he must order his guards to behead one of the prisoners, cook his head and bring it to him in a dish and eat it for dinner. All this must take place in front of the other prisoners. The cook will swap the head of the Zanji for that of a black sheep with the bones removed. In the general confusion, no-one will notice the exchange.

Alexander followed his teacher's counsel. Before the eyes of the Zanji prisoners, he ate the sheep's head with great relish. Playing his role, the commander sent orders to his cook that although up till then he had only been served with the heads of white people, - from now on he must cook only Zanji. I need no other dish, they are so tasty, - he declared.

When Alexander released the prisoners, they ran back to their camp to relate everything they had seen in his tent. Without allowing his enemies to recover from their shock, the Macedonian led them to the Zanji camp, riding at the head of his troops. It was a bloody battle. Driving a large caravan of elephants ahead of him into the ranks of the dark-skinned warriors, the startled animals charged deep into the enemy cohorts, trampling all in their path.

At the end of the battle, Alexander avenged Tutianush by ordering all his prisoners to be beheaded and left out for the vultures. They say that in the valley of caves, where the prisoners were put to death, the number of birds blotted out the sun, and everything left by the birds was carried away by ants through the burning desert.

This victory was so precious to Alexander that, instead of punishing the Zanji, he ordered a city to be built which would bear his name.

CHAPTER THIRTY NINE

Vengeance

Amongst scattered belongings in the camp, I found some scorched pages of our family Koran. I could mistake it for no other; it was a rare copy of the Koran, they don't make them like that anymore. But how had it ended up here?

I was stunned. For a minute I forgot about my pain, the war, and everything else. Another picture arose in my mind's eye. I saw my father returning home from the mosque on a rainy night. In an alleyway, the Arab or Doku or someone else lay in wait for him. Their faces were covered and hidden by darkness. They knocked the old man to the ground and began to kick him. They aimed their boots at his face, but Abdulaziz turned over and the blows landed on his shoulder.

The attackers said nothing but simply kicked hard at the old man. They tried to seize his Koran but Abdulaziz clutched it tightly. Then they struck his hands and pulled them away. Snatching the book from him, they ran off. Abdulaziz was left lying on the muddy ground with a broken shoulder and arm. He struggled to his feet and staggered home. No-one, including me, would know what had happened. Only now this picture unfolded before my eyes.

'It means Ginger told the truth,' I thought to myself.

Why would they attack the old man? Did they want to steal the precious Koran? I don't think so, more likely they wanted to punish Abdulaziz. Probably they wanted to make the attack look like a robbery. Abdulaziz's pride prevented him from admitting that someone had brutally attacked him, that someone had been able to knock him down and kick him. Now I realised why my father had been so anxious to get well. He wanted to recover so that he could deal with his attackers quietly and without fuss. My eyes burned, my hands shook violently. I couldn't control myself. I was close to a crisis of nerves. The Arab was nowhere to be seen. I sat down near one of the logs. From the depths of the forest I heard cries. I grabbed my gun but my hands shook so hard I couldn't hold it properly. I thought it was a unit of Russian paratroopers come to finish us off but, no, the Arab was dragging a Russian prisoner by his jacket and swearing at him. They came straight towards me. Two of our guys accompanied them. They had been on night patrol which had saved their lives.

– You all right? - one of the men called from afar. They could see my leg was covered in blood but they were more occupied with the soldier.

Al Rashid held a large knife in his right hand. Throwing the prisoner to the ground, he grabbed his hair. He wanted to lift his head up so he could cut the man's throat. The poor soldier guessed the Arab's intention. He lay on the ground and covered his head with his hands, and let out a blood-curdling wail.

– Cut him! - said one of our guys. - The Russian bastard will pay for this mess.

– Take your hands away, take your hands away, scum. You will die all the same, - the Arab shouted.

Our nerves were on edge, but the lad didn't give up. He wailed and kept holding on. Then Al Rashid stabbed his dagger into his arm. The first thrust was weak and only made a small cut in his hand. The second thrust went through his hand and struck his neck. The lad shook with pain and clutched his hand, leaving his neck exposed. Not losing a second, the Arab slit his throat in one swift move. Blood poured over the ground. The prisoner convulsed, his arms and legs shaking violently, but the Arab held his arms and knelt on his neck. Warm blood poured from the prisoner's throat, mingling with the earth.

I had to shoot the Arab. The moment had come. He wasn't paying any attention to me. But my hands shook so much I couldn't take aim. Straightening my good leg, I laid the gun on it and held it with my right hand. Taking aim as best I could, I let forth a volley of fire. The Arab fell and his body shuddered. The bullets had passed through him from his head to his kidneys. A thin stream of blood trickled through a tear in his field uniform. Two fighters jumped back and trained their weapons on me.

- Why did you do that? - one of them shouted. They were afraid to come near me and didn't know what to do in these circumstances - shoot or listen.

- He's my blood enemy, he murdered my father three months ago, - I said calmly, - I came here to get him.

- The fighters looked at me doubtfully.

- If anyone asks, tell them I shot him. Let them search for me.

My argument should have convinced them. Silence reigned. These lads didn't know me and were unsure what to do next. I had to say something to diffuse the tension so I threw my gun down. Judging by the expression on their faces, it helped a bit.

- We have to get out of here quickly, the Russians might show up, - I said, getting to my feet. - I live not far away. You can stay with me for a while until you decide where you are going next.

Supporting me under the arms, they carried me to my village. We walked for the whole day. Before we were halfway, my good leg had swollen up. I was hopping on it all the time and the weight had its effect, so every half hour I had to rest. During one of our halts, the two lads told me how the Arab survived the bombardment. Each morning, before Namaz, he inspected our posts. These lay at some distance from the camp and therefore, he was only knocked over by the blast. Doku had tied the prisoner to a tree on the far side of the camp. When the bomb hit the camp, the tree fell and burst into flames. The Russian was doubly lucky; the tree missed him when it fell, and then the flames burned through the ropes that bound him. He was a step away from freedom when Al Rashid caught him. All that happened after that, I already knew.

There was mourning in the village. Besides Doku, four of our village men had died in the camp. On discovering that three had returned alive, half the village gathered at my house. Everyone was asking what had happened up there in the mountains. We told them everything we had seen.

– It was some kind of Russian rocket, - said one of the older men.

– No, a NATO bomb fell on the camp by mistake, - said a second aksakkal. - They wanted to scare the Russians, they simply missed their mark.

Everything became clear when we found out that on that day the Russians directed their bombs at two other camps in the mountain. Such a delicate operation could only have been carried out through the use of satellites. I was sure the Russians had done this, and not NATO or the US, as the old men had so naively hoped.

Luckily our village doctor turned up and the room emptied very quickly. Bringing a basin of warm water, they cut off my trousers above the knees. When they washed away the blood, a bone could be seen protruding through the knee and my toes were turning black. The doctor didn't think for too long, but said I had to be taken to Shatoi straight away to get medical treatment. We only got hold of a car the next morning. By midday I was in the Shatoi district hospital. They injected me with something, then a grey-haired doctor came and said my situation was serious; they might have to amputate the leg.

– There are clear signs of gangrene and it spreads quickly, - said the doctor.

– No-one's going to amputate my leg, don't even think about it.

– That's what they all say, - the doctor replied in a calm voice. The doctor was an older man, so I could not answer him rudely. But his words and arrogance made me furious. He spoke as though he were going to amputate the leg of a dog or a cat, and he was talking about the operation without ceremony, right in front of his patient.

– Come and examine the leg again. Take more x-rays, take blood samples, skin, urine, sweat, whatever you like, - I shouted, and hurled a glass of water in the direction of the doctor and nurse. Then I pounded my fists against the wall and swore I would wreck the hospital if they cut off my leg.

The noise brought in some doctors from the next room. To calm me, they tried to inject me with something or other, but I wouldn't submit. Again I shouted that if they laid a finger on my leg, I'd blow them all up.

My hysterics had their effect on the doctors. Their arrogance and cynicism diminished. They operated. I had warned them that if I woke up and didn't see my leg, I'd shoot them all. The leg was in its place. They inserted a metal rod and hung a weight from it. They said they'd keep an eye on me for a couple of days. If my toes did not regain a normal appearance that would be it - the bones might grow together but the gangrene would rise higher.

Allah be praised! By the next day, my toes had already begun to take on a normal colour. Gradually my leg started to heal. I hoped it was a sign that one day luck would come back into my life.

CHAPTER FORTY

Ruslan

In January 1999 Russian forces seized the low-lying areas of the country without meeting any serious opposition. Many people understood that the outcome of the campaign would be decided in Grozny. All our forces gathered there.

On one of those cold nights the mothers of Ruslan and Emi came to our house. Over the past three years, practically since the day of my father's death, they had been frequent visitors to our house, trying to distract my mother from her sad thoughts. As I passed the veranda where they were sitting, I greeted them and asked about Emi and Ruslan. Ruslan's mother said she had no news of her son, and he had last been seen in Grozny. Emi's mother said her son was in Istanbul and had even married a Turkish woman. As she said these words, she glanced at me for a split second.

It was a look of judgement. I had no idea why it was aimed at me. Emi had never appeared in his homeland during the war years. He was involved in raising money for our fighters. He travelled in Europe, the countries of the near East, especially Jordan, where there was a large Chechen diaspora. Why should all problems be connected to me?

I slept very badly that night. Rising early in the morning I quietly gathered my things and set off to find Ruslan. As I left the village I came upon a group of refugees who had fled from Grozny. Since September the roads had been packed with refugees from the capital. The stream of human beings knew no end. They were all trying to reach the Baku-Rostov highway, which was constantly under Grad rocket-fire, and from there they would try to reach Ingushetia. At this critical juncture, only Ingushetia, Azerbaijan and Georgia were taking in Chechen refugees.

They said that the capital was being bombed day and night, even more relentlessly than during the first war. Grad rockets were destroying the roads, towns and villages through which both resistance fighters and civilians passed to leave the capital.

Heading along the Yarash Mardy - Dachu Berzoi - Duba Yurt highway, on the bridge over the Argun I saw a group of fighters. Many were wounded, their clothes torn and blood-stained. Over the past three days they had been retreating from Grozny away from the Russians. Some local residents and I helped them into a nearby house. They said that the Russians had drawn them to the west between Grozny and Alkhan Kala. A field around the bridge had been laid with special leaf mines. No-one saw them do this. Some said they were mines developed in a secret Ministry of Defence laboratory, and that they had been dropped by special planes. But they were extremely sensitive and could be triggered by a drop of rain. Shamil Basaev was blown up here.

– And what about Aslambek Ismailov? - asked someone standing near me. He had a strange accent and was obviously not a Chechen. When I turned to look at him, I saw a bald man of about forty with glasses.

– Aslambek is dead. So are Lecha Dudaev and Khunkap Pasha Israpilov. Many of our leaders are dead. Shamil was wearing American-made anti-mine boots and they saved his life, but the others rest on the field of battle.

– Can you get through to Grozny now? - the foreigner asked.

Everyone in the room stared at him. What was a foreigner from some peaceful place in Europe or America doing in this God-forsaken land? Why had he gone into the hell of battle, and how did he know the names of our commanders?

– You won't get further than Duba Yurt. They are bombing that village relentlessly. There's hardly a single house left.

– And who are you? - one of the fighters finally enquired.

– I'm a journalist, - he held out a paper to the man who had asked the question.

"Thomas Goltz"[21] – the man read aloud. But learning the stranger's name failed to dispel our doubts. Who this American was - a genuine journalist, a spy or simply a madman, I never found out.

I left the house and decided to help the wounded fighters. Everyone was needed now. Hobbling on my injured leg, I hurried to join those who were trying to help them. Before we could manage to carry all the wounded into a house, a massive bombardment from Grad missiles began. Several houses collapsed as though made of cardboard, scattering red tiles for dozens of metres. The fighters could no longer move. All who had the strength took shelter in basements. An hour later the firing ceased.

The owner of the house brought us food and water. It seemed that, regardless of the bombardment, she had gone to the kitchen and cooked chicken for the fighters. Everyone tucked into the food. Having eaten, some of the fighters fell asleep for a couple of hours. I started to ask around for news of Ruslan. Some fighters said that he had left the capital with everyone else. They were not in his unit and did not know what had become of him.

– We should go either towards Vedeno or the Argun Gorge, - said a short man. - We should leave in a couple of hours in order to reach the next village by morning.

We set off that night. There were about forty men in the unit, not more. One group decided to go to Ulus Kert and I went with the other towards the village of Yarysh Mardy. Yarysh Mardy was famous because the Khattab unit destroyed

---

21 Thomas Goltz is a renowned US journalist who covered the massacre in Samashki village, Chechnya in April 1995.

a large Russian convoy there in 1996. Around a hundred soldiers were killed, and twenty-five military vehicles destroyed. In Ulus Kert, the celebrated Pskov division was utterly routed.

We headed through a tract of forest along the right bank of the Argun River, following the old road which ran practically parallel to the highway. We walked very quietly; no-one smoked or chatted.

At about four in the morning, we reached the outskirts of Yarysh Mardy. We looked at the first house. - Everything seems to be quiet here, - said our leader, a bit too loudly. He was trying to speak above the noise of the Argun River which flowed close by.

We did not enter the first house as we feared a trap. Going a little further, we entered a nondescript-looking house. The inhabitants greeted us in a friendly way, but cautiously. The family had a lot of children, and everyone was running feverishly from room to room. We sat down in the courtyard. The householders brought us hot tea.

— Is there a doctor among you? - our host asked.

We exchanged glances. No, there was no doctor among us.

— We can give first aid if someone is wounded, - said our leader.

— Three of our men came here last night. They were escaping from the Russians who had held them prisoner, but one of them had his eye put out. He is losing blood, we don't know what to do. He is unconscious.

There was nothing we could do to help. Our leader went into the room where the wounded man lay and came out again to the courtyard a couple of minutes later.

— He probably won't last till morning. He's very pale.

Towards morning the lad died. When I and several other fighters went into the house to bring out the body, I saw his older brother, who had remained by his side all the time, embracing the dead man's head and weeping. Approaching him, I touched his shoulder so that I could pick up the body. As soon as he felt my touch, the brother embraced the body more closely. He twitched violently as though I had come to kill him. I felt dreadful.

We left the room and waited another half hour. Finally the older brother emerged and asked for help in carrying the corpse. He said they were from a small hamlet in the Shtoum Kale district. Their family cemetery was in the village and the shaheed must be buried there. It was impossible to find a car. No-one dared to drive along the roads. For a long time we tried to persuade the man to bury his brother in the local cemetery but he would not agree.

The third man, who had escaped from the Russians with the two brothers, was taciturn. He was probably still in shock after spending four days and nights under fire from the Russians. We were all from the same district and so I asked them about Ruslan.

–   It was because of him that we were able to escape, - said the fighter, suddenly reviving.

–   But where is he? - I asked, unable to believe my ears.

–   I don't know, - the man wavered.

Intuitively, I realised I was about to hear something terrible. I led the man off to one side and, clutching at him, I demanded he tell me everything he knew. And so he told me that they had been surrounded on the southern edge of Grozny in Chernorechki. The Russians were in front of them and behind them was the Grozny lake. There was nowhere to run, and Ruslan had already been wounded in the chest. When the Russians searched them for weapons, they found the flag of Ichkeria beneath Ruslan's clothes, tied around his waist. It was what the Russians needed. Everyone who had been wounded almost to the point of death, was made to get to their feet and stand in a line. Ruslan was supported by his comrades. The Russian soldiers and officers began to spit on our flag, then they brought it Ruslan. As he was the highest ranking officer in the army of Ichkeria, they wanted to humiliate him before the others so that they could see what the highlanders' hero was really made of.

And what do you think he did? Ruslan snatched the dirty and spat-upon flag of Ichkeria and began to kiss it. The other fighters, exhausted and shattered as they were, were inflamed by Ruslan's action. With bare hands they threw themselves on the Russians. Most of them were cut down by machine-gun fire, but several were able to escape in the confusion. But what had happened to Ruslan after that, he didn't know.

...I learned of his fate later in our village. As I reached home, three days of mourning had just ended. I went straight to Ruslan's house. On seeing me, Uncle Jamal could not contain himself. - They tied him to two tanks and pulled him apart, - he said, - Then they dragged his body behind a tank for several days in revenge.

Uncle Jamal cried his heart out like a baby. I cried too; something died in me that day, something very holy, very good, unselfish and noble, like Ruslan himself.

My thoughts often turn to that young man. Whenever I remember myself as I was, Ruslan and Emi are beside me. We had so many adventures and got into many scrapes through silliness and naivety. I remember how he drank so much kvass[22] that had been brought into the village that he messed his trousers. At the time we were up on the mountain and he slid down on his backside so the soiled trousers could not be seen. For him to show that he had shat his pants would have been worse than death. Or how we wrapped ourselves in white sheets and climbed through Emi's window at night. As a very religious boy, Emi was scared

---

22 Kvass is a soft drink made from fermented rye bread

of ghosts and evil spirits. We wanted to scare him by appearing as phantoms. However, we climbed through the window of his little sisters' room and scared them to death. After that, we swore to ourselves that we wouldn't joke with religion. Or the time when we were still quite little, when we climbed out onto the roof of his house with some toy wings. We were going to fly, but when I saw how high up we were I refused. Ruslan jumped and broke both his legs...

For many years afterwards, I would often see visions of his last minutes, how they attached him half dead to the tanks, how he groaned with pain, how the rope started to pull. I saw his flushed face, his dirty hair stuck to his forehead and the fire in his eyes which no force in the world could extinguish. Another second and the tanks had torn Ruslan in two. I knew exactly what Ruslan had thought about in the last moments of his life - that quiet and humble woman who had jumped into the flames to save him in far-off childhood.

CHAPTER FORTY ONE

The Deaths of Alexander and Nizami

'Why am I feeling so terrible?' Alexander kept asking himself all along the road back to Rum. He was neither wounded nor sick, but with each day he felt weaker. In the small town of Shakhrazura he began to feel really ill. The Commander suspected that he had been poisoned, and he sent his emissary to fetch Aristotle, asking him to bring all the doctors he could find. When the wise man reached his student's tent, he found Alexander in torment. Checking his pulse, Aristotle explained this malady as a simple illness, and ordered a herbal remedy to be prepared. But in his heart, the philosopher said to himself, 'Not even the water of life will save him if the day of departure has come.'

Nothing would help, and Alexander knew this. At the end of the day, he asked for a mirror to be brought to him. He gazed at the image of an emaciated man whose soul had almost left the flesh. He called everyone to his deathbed and bid them farewell. Aristotle, Bulinas, Plato, Valis, Farfori and others stood around his bed.

He praised each one and recalled every battle, how they had beheaded the mighty Fura, defeated Chaipal in China, avenged Kabila and Habila, plunged Ferdun into the flames, reached the holy circle of the Kaaba[23] and everywhere proclaimed, "fate will protect us." But not this time.

– He who enters the door of life will see a second door which he can't avoid,
  believe me - he said to his faithful servants with sadness.

---

23 In Nizami's era it was prohibited to write about any ancient heroes apart from Alexander of Macedonia. An exception was made for him as he is mentioned in the Koran. Nizami and subsequent renowned Islamic poets show him as a warrior spreading the Islamic faith, even though there was no Islam in Alexander's time. Chapters in Iskandername show Alexander as defending and disseminating Islam.

He also asked to be buried naked because he had been born naked, but his final request was the most important. Alexander asked that just before his death, some earth that he had taken from the land of darkness should be placed in his fist. Wherever you are, whatever great deeds you have accomplished, however many riches you have, you will take no more than this to the next world. That was the thinking behind the gesture. And so, the next morning, Alexander of Macedonia passed away.

His followers decided to bury him in Egypt, which was relatively peaceful. The death of the student also killed the teacher. Following Alexander, Aristotle also passed away. And then Plato, Valis, Bulinas and other faithful generals.

This was Nizami's last work. He died at the age of 63 without finishing the final chapter, which had been intended to sing the praises of the man who commissioned the book. The poet was buried in a vault with honours such as those bestowed upon his hero, Alexander. But unlike Alexander's, his grave has lasted to this day, surviving invasions by Mongols, Arabs, Persians and Russian aggressors.

The writer's legacy would be magnificent. Monuments would be erected to him in all corners of the medieval world. His works would be widely read and they would help people overcome difficulties and hardships, like those of that old beggar who I met in Ganja at Nizami's tomb. But these days people like him were drops in the ocean.

Some people live their whole lives without finding answers to the most important questions of our existence but the poet wrote many short but brilliant couplets to address these. For example:

Without love, no seed will grow. Only in homes where there is peace, love and goodwill.

Or this second couplet, which characterises those such as Al Rashid very well:

Not every servant of God is faithful. A servant who loves only himself is a wastrel.

The great poet dispensed wise advice for so many of life's situations. As for me, my favourite was an aphorism inscribed on his grave:

If all you send me is trouble and grief, let me discover what that gift will teach.

And the Lord certainly sent me an unusual gift.

CHAPTER FORTY TWO

The eyes of Abdulaziz

Why was my mother so excited when I reached home at last? She was not laughing, nor jumping for joy, but I could see that she was quietly happy about something. That evening, I had a bite to eat and went to sleep. When I opened my eyes in the morning I almost fell out of bed. My mother stood beside me with a baby in her arms.

— Just don't tell me I've done the wrong thing, - she said.

— And don't tell me I'm going out of my mind! She reminds me of Father.

— That's why I took her in; just look at her eyes! They are those of Abdulaziz.

Indeed this tiny being looked at me with the eyes of my father. The resemblance was uncanny. At first I could not believe it. I thought that my imagination was playing tricks. It was a good job my mother confirmed the resemblance.

— I've named her Fatima, in honour of the prophet Mohammed's beloved daughter, - my mother continued. - She will be beloved in our family, just as Fatima was the soul of the prophet's family. What's more, as she is a gift from Allah, we have to give her a name worthy of the Almighty.

My mother spoke as all the village women do, convinced of her arguments. No-one could persuade her that the appearance of Fatima in our home was most likely a result of the cataclysmic upheaval in our country, rather than a gift from God. But who was I to present my case to? Ayna would never agree with me, and Fatima's eyes also went against me. And it is impossible not to have faith in eyes.

All this talk of religion sometimes produces strange thoughts, even in me. For example, it sometimes seemed to me that Fatima resembled the smallest angel in Islam, Rizvan. According to our canon, Rizvan stands at the gates of paradise and admits those who will dwell there for eternity. It seemed right that the little Fatima, with her tiny carefree and merry face, should greet the inhabitants of paradise.

But how had she appeared at our house? Who were her parents and how long would she remain with us? Refugees from Grozny who were passing through our village on the way to Georgia, gave her to my mother. They had come across her entirely by accident; no-one knew who she was or where she came from. A child without family or tribe, as my father would have said.

Such details quickly became irrelevant. Her laughter, enigmatic expressions and pugnacious character, which clearly showed even though she was so young, became the pivot around which our household revolved. My mother would call me to look at how Fatima beat her feet on the floor, or how she held up her hands and laughed wildly when my mother pulled faces at her.

Fatima's laughter was so powerful and bewitching that it made you forget all your troubles. But at the end of June, a unit of Russians arrived in the village. There were no more than thirty of them, and their leader entered the village alone. He walked into the centre and had a talk with the elders. He said they wouldn't harm anyone; they had orders to control the road that led to Georgia.

In the evening, I went to the elders to find out how they would respond. They were divided; some said we should attack the Russians, others that we should admit them into the village.

–   There are few of them, they won't do anything to us, - said one of the elders. - Let them think that they are keeping an eye on us and we'll keep an eye on them.

–   And what if our sons are arrested because of them? What shall we do then? How will we answer for this? - asked one of the aksakkals.

– They won't, they're not idiots, they know that we'll cut them off in the mountains before they can call for help. Let them think they're watching us, and we'll watch them. Everything must remain calm and peaceful.

The Russians didn't appear to be idiots either. It was no accident that they chose precisely our village to hole up in. When one of our fighters approached the village, the same officer who had first spoken to us went to have a talk with him. He said that this was his territory and no-one could pass. If the fighters tried to break through, the Russians would slaughter everyone in the village. And so we co-existed, pretending that we didn't trouble one another.

In a couple of months, my tension diminished. The soldiers began to pay visits to some of the villagers and walk around unarmed. But this calm frightened me. My intuition told me that as soon as the delicate balance of power in the village was shifted, then the Russians would wipe us all out. We knew what they had done in the larger villages of Sirzhin-Yurt and Komsomolsk where, with no explanation, they took young men hostage, tortured and killed them. If their relatives paid, they let them go, but if not they killed them. In Chechnya, bodies earn a higher ransom than living people. It is considered a great sin not to give a family member an orthodox burial.

– Mother, with my injured leg they won't hesitate. They'll say I'm a terrorist, a Wahhabi, a member of the underground resistance, and that will be that. We'll have to leave Chechnya, - I said to Ayna one evening.

– How can we? We can't leave father's grave. Who will look after it? - she hesitated.

– You're thinking of father, but if we don't leave now we stand a good chance of ending up beside him. If they take me tomorrow, you won't be able to pay the ransom. Neither you nor the neighbours have any money. We have one scrawny cow left. Without her milk, Fatima wouldn't last long, and so you couldn't sell the cow to ransom me. If we leave now, we have a chance of survival.

My mother thought for a while. I didn't know what she would say to me but I had already decided that I would go nowhere without her. Under no circumstances would I leave if she insisted on staying. For fear of being taken hostage by the Russians was only part of the truth. The other part was that I wanted to see the world and, if I was lucky, discover my true vocation. How could I find myself if there is no-one left in this village to accompany me on my path? And let's say I did find my calling - who would there be to appreciate it? I loved and respected these backward villagers, but they were tiny drops in the ocean. I was young, naive and romantic, and so I thought I could make my mark in a more worldly environment.

Ayna said yes. Closing the shutters and giving the cow to our neighbours, we set off in the direction of Georgia. I phoned ahead to Emi to tell him that I was coming to Istanbul, but I did not tell him the reason. I didn't want to scare him with my radical plans.

We climbed higher and higher until we could no longer see the luxuriant meadows. When we saw the lovely Mount Balboa, we realised we were close to Georgia. I looked back for the last time. A cascade of beautiful mountain peaks bid me farewell. I was gazing on this fairytale landscape perhaps for the last time. Perhaps I would never again see my house, the village, the river and the mountains, which probably have no equals in the world. No one and nowhere could replace all this. I decided not to look back any longer and not think about the Caucasus until I reached the villages of Kistinskii.

And so I walked on for a couple of minutes, but I couldn't control myself and I looked back. This would really be for the last time. My eyes filled with tears. I would like to say how much I loved and would continue to love all and everything in this tiny corner of the world. But as I remembered all and everything, for some reason I cried out, - Farewell, unwashed Russia ...[24]

---

24 From a poem by Lermontov, written in 1840 or 1841, in connection with his exile to the Caucasus

CHAPTER FORTY THREE

Istanbul

It only took a day and a night to reach Istanbul from Tbilisi. Around four in the afternoon we alighted from the bus to embrace Emi. He had changed, matured, and become very Europeanised. He had come to meet me in unusual white jeans and he had half a kilo of gel rubbed into his hair. You'd never have thought that he'd come here to study the word of God. He took us through the centre of the city, which swarmed like a hive of bees. On some square or other I saw a large circular monument with a flock of pigeons sitting around it. No-one caught them or shot them. The birds felt so secure that they even ate out of people's hands. In Grozny, people lived in fear of their lives, and here all creatures felt safe.

We crossed over a huge bridge which Emi explained linked two continents, Asia and Europe. From here on, our journey lay on the Asiatic side of the city.

— First let's get you settled, and then we'll look for work for you. It's the loveliest city on earth, - Emi spoke in snatches, between shouting at taxi drivers who were trying to cut us up. The city traffic was utterly chaotic. Everyone was flashing their lights and trying to surge ahead. Emi had to brake hard every couple of minutes, and he shouted and gesticulated whenever some driver annoyed him.

While he drove and cursed the drivers all around us Emi told us that he had ended his involvement with the Chechen diaspora and gone into business. He exported clothing to Kazakhstan, where there was oil wealth and a large Chechen society. - I don't want to become disillusioned any more, especially over such important matters as patriotism and honour. Foreigners all talk about their love for us, but in practice they only look after their own baser ends.

That was all he was able to say to me about his six years of agitational work which he had carried out in Turkey and several west European countries.

Towards the evening, we arrived in the Sultanbeyli district. This part of Istanbul was quite different from the European side. Mean alleyways with two-storey houses drowning in filth; dishevelled children and women in the hijab on the streets. There was an air of depression here. I had supposed that all Istanbul was as beautiful as Taksim.

– This a gecekondu[25]. – an area of houses put up without permission, - said Emi, as though reading my thoughts. - Several Chechen families live here. You can turn to them if you have any problems.

The flat which he had rented consisted of a single room and a kitchen. It was empty. There were not even any knives, forks or glasses. It seems that here they rent out homes without furniture or utensils. There was nowhere even to lay little Fatima down. Emi had paid the rent for three months. Bidding us a hasty goodbye, he left. My mother and I looked at each other. What were we to do? We only had a little money and we had to buy a few basics at least. Leaving my mother with Fatima, I went out to look for a shop where I could buy food and cooking pots, plates and cutlery.

I found a shop close by where I could buy everything I needed quite cheaply. When I returned, we made tea and gave Fatima a cup of milk. We lay down by the wall and prepared to go to sleep. Just then, someone knocked at the door. Emi had returned with two Turks.

– Did you think I'd deserted you? - he smiled. They brought a table and chairs into the flat, a small rug, an inflatable bed and a box with fruit and other food. My mother was in seventh heaven as she thanked Emi and the others. I accepted it all as our due. As my friend, he could not have acted otherwise.

---

25 Gecekondu – is a Turkish word meaning "built overnight"

Slowly but surely, we began to feel at home in that world of contrasts. Getting up early in the morning, I would cross to the European side of the Bosphorus and walk the streets of Istanbul, thinking about what I might do until I found a regular job. With each day our funds diminished, and I had heard nothing more from my friend. By the end of the first week we had to economise drastically, except where Fatima was concerned. For her there were no limits. As I left home early in the morning and returned late in the evening, there was no need to cook dinner for me. I began to lose a lot of weight.

I was prepared to take any kind of work, sweeping the streets, selling trinkets or pies, or anything else that came up. At first I thought about souvenirs, but for that you had to invest a minimum of a thousand dollars, which was all we had left. I could not risk sinking it all into such a project. Life itself came up with an answer. The day was hot and every second passer-by carried a bottle of water. Water cost a few kopeks and did not require much outlay.

In one of the rubbish bins beside the Hotel Sheraton, in an area of large private houses, I found a big black suitcase. It was old and dirty. I dragged it home through the whole city and washed it with water and shampoo. After that, it began to look more respectable. I lined the inside of the case with plastic bags to make it watertight. My mother did not understand what I was doing.

– My business in Turkey begins with this black suitcase, - I proudly announced.

– Who will buy that old case from you? - my mother said sympathetically.

– Not the case, mother, but what I am going to sell from out of it. From this moment on I shall become like a clever Chinese. They all become millionaires from selling small items. In ten years' time, I will be selling cars, planes and computers. Until then I will amass capital. My mother only nodded, as though unwilling to get caught up in my fantasies.

I went to the nearest shop and bought a case of water bottles and a couple of two-kilogram boxes of ice. There were 38 bottles in the case. I had to lay out six dollars altogether, four for water and two for the ice. I planned to sell each bottle for fifty cents, so that my return on investment would be three hundred per cent. Or so I thought, until I made the journey to Topkapi, the palace of the Turkish sultans, it took me two hours to get there, I had to change buses twice and also take a ferry. That cost a dollar and a half. And then the suitcase full of water was a nightmare to carry. I couldn't hold it by the handle in case it broke off and then it would be quite useless. I had to balance it on my shoulder. Also, the tourists were not as stupid as I had thought. No-one wanted to pay fifty cents for water. They all wanted the bottles at half price which I could not agree to. My competitors on the other hand, who were many, and who sold a thousand other things besides water, such as souvenirs, sunglasses and so on, willingly gave discounts. Their wares looked more hygienic than mine, laid out on clean stalls and in special cases in which they could put ice and not worry about it melting. They looked on me with undisguised scorn, as though thinking, 'Where did that lowlife come from? He can't even speak Turkish'. And then another problem emerged. I laid the bottles beneath the ice, which soon melted. It turned out that you had to do the opposite - lay the bottles on top of the ice which would protect it from the sun's rays.

In a word, after two hours my business sank like the bottles into the depths of the suitcase. Fire burned within me, a hurricane raged, rivers burst their banks, as shame and hopelessness overwhelmed me.

My first customer was a black American woman. She handed me a dollar note and while I was searching for change, she took another bottle. 'She probably felt sorry for me,' I thought. Then two Turkish girls approached and bought bottles. By evening I had sold seven bottles, taking three and a half dollars. If you count the journey, which cost another dollar and a half, then my net takings amounted to fifty cents. I had stood in the sun for a whole day just to earn fifty cents.

On the second day, after selling two bottles in total, I decided to throw in the towel. I would sell the remaining bottles and finish with it all. But it happened to be the weekend, which turned out to be the busiest time for trading. Saturday proved successful for me. For the first time since I had arrived in the city I was able to speak Russian. A middle-aged couple from Yaroslavl bought water and I struck up a conversation with them. They were poring over their map, trying to find their way to Agia Sofia, although it was only two paces away. After a couple of minutes a large tour group joined them and they bought fifteen bottles in all. Water was the least of their needs. Married couples wanted to know where to find the cheapest bazaars and young single people, where they could find the best entertainment.

— Friends, - I enthused, - it's very easy to ascertain prices in the market. Simply halve the one they give you and then you'll have roughly the right price. Barter till your last breath, otherwise they simply won't understand you.

The Russian tourists stared at me as though I was a priest celebrating Mass on a holy day.

Some wanted to buy women, so I named a non-existent street and even 'showed them' how to get there. My conversation with the tourists attracted the attention of my competitors. One of them, under the pretext of buying water, came over and asked who I was and where I came from. In my broken Turkish, I explained how I ended up here, with neither family nor clan. The news that I was a Chechen spread like wildfire. Many of the other traders came over to shake my hand, some hugged me. Everyone spoke warmly about our war with the Russians and their two eighteenth century wars against the Tsar's troops. They affirmed the brotherhood of the Caucasian Peoples. This was all very pleasant, but to say that I was part of a brotherhood with my competitors was not really true. It was all hot air.

The next day, when I arrived at Topkapi with my famous suitcase, the traders gave me an old white container from which they used to sell water. They also gave me an umbrella that had seen better days. I was very grateful for the torn umbrella; standing in the hot sun all day had given me the appearance of a Moor. From that moment on, things took a turn for the better. Each day I sold an average of two boxes of water and my Turkish improved. 'Force of circumstance and the need to earn a living are the best methods for learning a language,' I said to myself. After a long day, I dropped into a cheap cafe, like one of our snack bars, and ate an 'iskander' kebab and drank ayran. Buying food and drink for my family, I returned home, where my mother and Fatima were waiting with a delicious dinner. Fatima would delight us all with her merry antics.

– The weather will turn in a couple of weeks, people will buy less water, - said the moustachioed Ibrahim, one of the Topkapi traders.

– What can I do then?

– You need a small stall like those we have, from which you can display souvenirs, t-shirts, sunglasses and ladies' handbags.

I had watched Ibrahim and the other traders sell these goods like hot cakes. He proposed that we go into business together. I would go to Antalya, which we nicknamed 'Russian Dacha' because of the masses of Russian tourists it attracted. I could buy goods wholesale there, straight from the factories and not from the middlemen in Istanbul, as Ibrahim and his companions usually did. In two months I had saved my first thousand dollars.

I worked the whole day long, often without lunch. Ibrahim came and went, each time finding reasons for his absence. And each time he came he seemed nervous. At first I thought he had domestic problems and these would blow over, but his wrath intensified and he would blow up for no reason over small issues. For example, if a white t-shirt on the stall got stained or if I changed money for tourists. - A golden rule of trading is never to change money for people, - he repeated each time. He was right, because sometimes it left me without enough change to give a customer, and then they would go to another stall. But the way he spoke made me angry, and it got worse. Sometimes he arrived with his friends and began to lecture me on how to serve customers. Then I would answer him quite rudely. When he really leant on me, I told him where to go.

'Why has Ibrahim changed from a friendly and cheerful lad to an angry dog?' This question worried me a good deal, for our business was doing well and the wholesalers in Antalya were pleased with our custom. It all became clear when the police showed up one day. They put me in handcuffs and took me to the station. I had no permit to trade and they began to threaten me.

— We'll call the Russian consulate and hand you over. The Russians will stitch you up on charges of terrorism or kidnapping, and they'll display you on TV as a captured terrorist. Then you'll wise up.

— Before you do that, hundreds of my relatives throughout Turkey will descend on this place. They'll riot and smash everything in their path, and ordinary people will spit in your face for handing me over to those butchers. - I shouted.

— You scum! - the policeman grabbed me by the collar and threw me against the wall, injuring my head. Warm liquid seeped through my hair. Then more cops arrived, alerted by the noise of our altercation. These mountain goats were merciless; they kicked me with all their might. I rolled into a ball and tried to protect my head with my arm. Giving me a few blows to my sides, legs and kidneys, they lifted me up and punched my face several times. One of the blows hit me in the ear which began to ring.

Then they grabbed my arms and legs, and dragged me into a single cell. Only towards evening did they allow me to make a phone call. I rang Emi who came to collect me. When I told him how I'd ended up in the police station, he immediately concluded that Ibrahim had denounced me.

— It often happens here. The Turks love us, that's a fact. But this is a capitalist country and money is God. Get used to it.

– I grafted for two months for that bastard, and I'll flatten him if he doesn't pay what he owes me.

– He has paid that to the police already, or at least a part of it. If you show your face there again, they could deport you. Forget about Ibrahim. There's enough shit like him in this place.

– Is that the best you can advise? - I asked, annoyed.

– Yes, - he answered, and burst out laughing. - You're not in the Caucasus now where you can take your revenge.

CHAPTER FORTY FOUR

Fatima

I recovered quickly from my first unsuccessful attempt to be a trader in the beautiful city of Istanbul. 'To hell with all that,' I said to myself. 'I'd never make a trader in any case.' What's more, Istanbul was quite a cheerful place and in this environment my own worries and disappointment became easier to bear. The city of fourteen million inhaled the peaceful air of Uskudare, Beyoglu and Sultanbeyli and loudly exhaled the cacophony of taxi drivers, traders, police, tourists and criminals in Taksim and Beshik Tash.

The most important lesson from the Ibrahim saga was not to take words at face value, no matter how sincere and pleasing they seem, but press ahead until you find your own situation and calling. A couple of days later, Emi told me that a small hotel, Mega Residence, was looking for a washer-up. It was in the Besiktas district. When I reached the hotel, it transpired that it was not a permanent position. They only needed me when they held banquets, and had a pile of plates, glasses, knives and forks that was too big for the regular staff to handle. A big plus was the fact that in one night I could earn as much as I had in three or four days' trading outside Topkapi.

After I had worked three or four times at the hotel Burak, the manager, began to call me in more often. He was an unusually intelligent young man, and a born manager. For example, in the mornings, when guest from cold countries in Europe such as Scandinavia and the Balkans were due to sign out, he would put up a sign announcing the temperature in Istanbul. Depending on the situation, he would add or subtract a few degrees. When the guest saw that he was leaving a warm country for Finland where it was minus twenty-five, or Sweden where it was snowing, he often changed his mind and decided to stay a few days longer. The trick worked especially well with older couples who were living out their days comfortably on a pension.

But his enterprise was useless where Russian guests were concerned. They were a special category and took up eighty per cent of the manager's energy. Most of the Russians stole everything they could lay their hands on; towels, shampoo, slippers ... And each morning he had to replenish the buffet three times. Most of the hotel's guests just ate breakfast and went out for the day, but some Russians ate and then went back to the buffet and made sandwiches which they munched on contentedly as they explored the city. Burak said they would soon be ruined by clients like that.

Washing up was not a pleasant job, especially having to wash the grease and fat off several hundred plates in one night. In order to kill time, I bought a personal cassette player and recorded the best known Caucasian dance music on it, such as Lezginka and Kartuli songs. So I washed dishes with my hands, and my legs instinctively moved to the tunes. My injured leg still hurt but I tried to ignore the pain. All in all it was entertaining. So much fun that I didn't notice one of the hotel's employees record me on a video camera as I danced. In an hour, the video clip was the hit of the hotel. People passed it to one another so they could watch the hot-blooded highlander show off his agility. One after another, the waiters, cleaners and kitchen hands came to ask me to dance the Lezginka for them. That dance was exotica for them and sent them into ecstasy. - In our dances we move our arms or our legs but not both together. It's unbelievable the way you move both together - said the Turks in one voice.

They say that where there is bad then good will follow. Losing my job as a street trader gave me more time to devote to my family. Fatima celebrated her first birthday, and was already walking. As soon as I returned home she would open her arms and beat her legs on the floor, demanding that I pick her up to play with her. The more time I spent at home, the more attached she became to me. Sometimes it was hard to leave the house. She followed me to the door and wouldn't let me out. When my mother came to the rescue to take her back into the room, she began to cry loudly. - Don't take any notice of her tears, go about your business - said my mother sternly. But all the same, I could not leave Fatima to cry, and I would return, only for her to burst into tears again as I left a minute later.

I usually took her to the park every Saturday and Sunday. Fatima went mad with joy when she saw a bird, a cat or a dog. She would throw herself at them and fearlessly pull cats by their tails or ears. One Sunday I took her to a place called Sariyer near the Bosphorus. There they sold fish kebabs. We walked for a whole day through the lovely woods and narrow streets of Sariyer. Fresh air and exercise had their effect. Towards evening, Fatima fell asleep in my arms.

It was already growing dark. I sat on a bench and stared at the waters of the Bosphorus and the Dardenelle straits. It was here that two currents met, throwing up intriguing patterns on the surface, as though each current wanted to show the other who was stronger. Little waves formed and were instantly swallowed by larger ones. Fatima slept in my arms and, as always, stroked my ear. Her warm little breaths tickled my neck. It was a pleasant feeling.

I didn't look great, my face sprouted stubble and my clothes and boots were worn and shabby. Perhaps some people took me for a bum. But as they walked by everyone without exception threw me a scarcely perceptible smile because of Fatima. At that moment I was the happiest person alive and it was all because of my daughter. That tiny creature clasped me softly, giving me a sense of being needed. Far in the distance I could see a launch with lifebelts attached to its side. It was the ferry that would take us back to Sultanbeyli. My eyes followed the boat, while before my mind's eye there appeared my father, Ruslan, Faizul... I sensed their souls flying around me, close by.

***

I know that my story, which began ten years ago, is drawing to its close. The reader will never know what happens to me, my mother or little Fatima. Not tomorrow, not in a month's time, not in a year... All that remains are a couple of lines in which to write the most important words. Which words are these? First, I must avenge Ruslan and Faizul, that's for sure. But is that the most important matter? No. I must become a respected man, as Abdulaziz wished. True, but that's not the most important thing either. The most important thing that I want to share in this story of my journey from the peaks of the High Caucasus to the shores of Istanbul, is the question of how long I will live, and what I will live for. Why do I want to answer that question? I don't know – it just seems the most important one that I face.

I would like to live to see Fatima grow into a beautiful, proud, confident and happy woman. I want to give her the best education and help her build a good life for herself. I want to help her choose a good man for her husband and I want to live to the day when her children will be able to care for her and protect her as I do now. And then I will be able to die in peace.

Of course, Fatima doesn't know all this. She grips my ear with her fingers, and sleeps peacefully. I just want to live, and go on living...

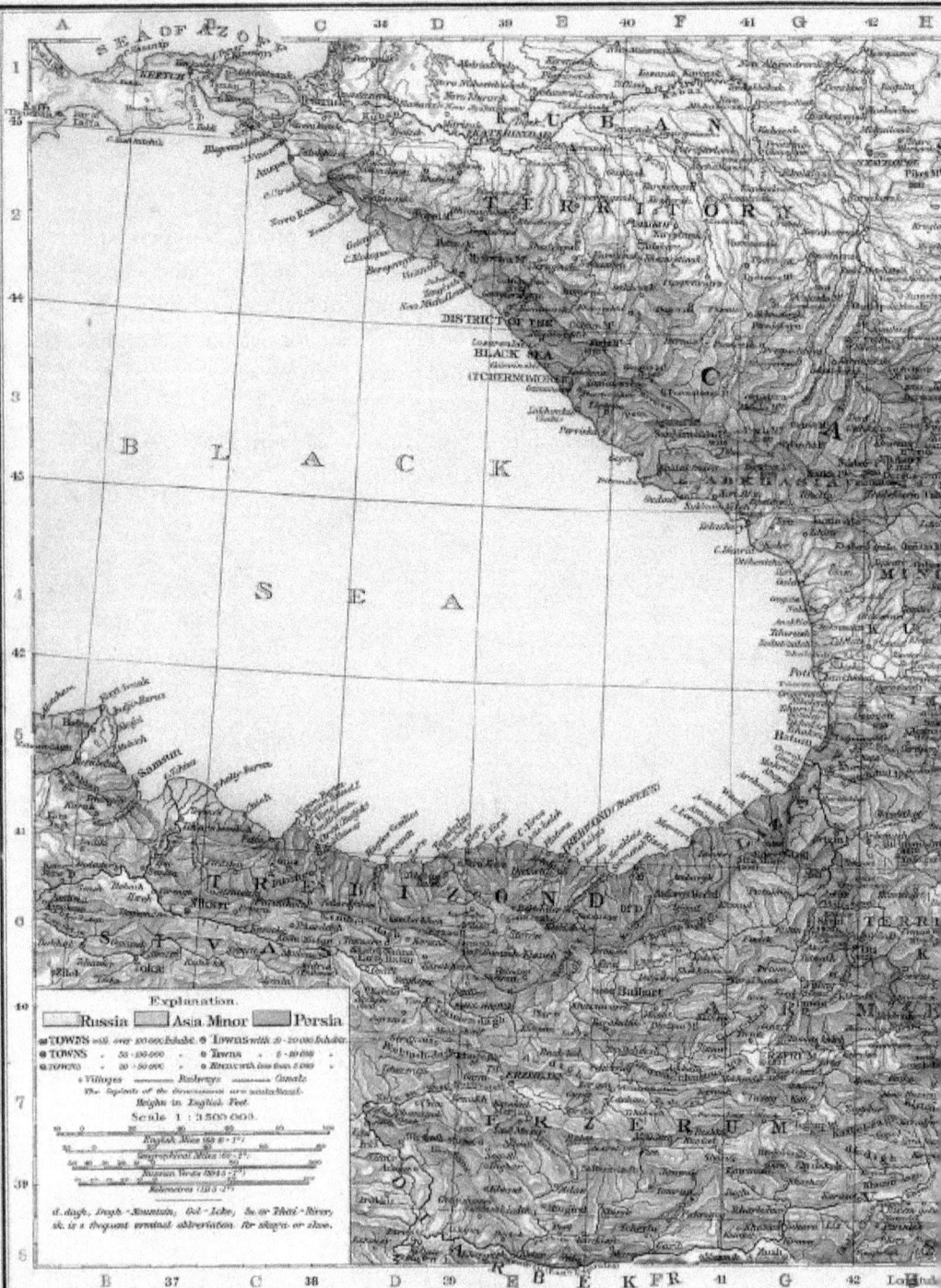

SEA OF AZOFF

BLACK SEA

KUBAN TERRITORY

DISTRICT OF THE BLACK SEA (TCHERNOMORIE)

TREBIZOND

SIVAS

ERZERUM

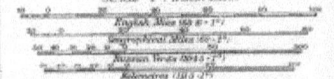

Explanation.

Russia   Asia Minor   Persia

Scale 1 : 3.500.000.

ASTRAKHAN

VROPOL

Georgievsk

Steppe of the
Karz-Nogai

CASPIAN

SEA

Petrovsk

15 Feet below the Level of the Black Sea

FREE TERRITORY

TERRITORY

DAGHESTAN

Derbend

TIFLIS

GEORGIA

SHIRVAN

ELIZABETPOL

BAKU

ERIVAN

Erivan

KARABAGH

Manisshlak
Peninsula

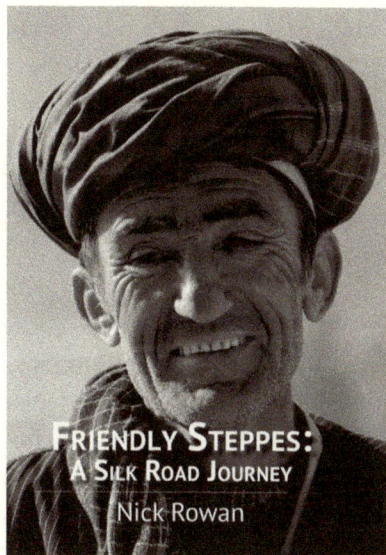

Friendly Steppes: A Silk Road Journey by Nick Rowan

This is the chronicle of an extraordinary adventure that led Nick Rowan to some of the world's most incredible and hidden places. Intertwined with the magic of 2,000 years of Silk Road history, he recounts his experiences coupled with a remarkable realisation of just what an impact this trade route has had on our society as we know it today. Containing colourful stories, beautiful photography and vivid characters, and wrapped in the local myths and legends told by the people Nick met and who live along the route, this is both a travelogue and an education of a part of the world that has remained hidden for hundreds of years.

Friendly Steppes: A Silk Road Journey reveals just how rich the region was both culturally and economically and uncovers countless new friends as Nick travels from Venice through Eastern Europe, Iran, the ancient and modern Central Asia of places like Samarkand, Bishkek and Turkmenbashi, and on to China, along the Silk Roads of today.

RRP:£14.95
ISBN: 978-0-9557549-4-4

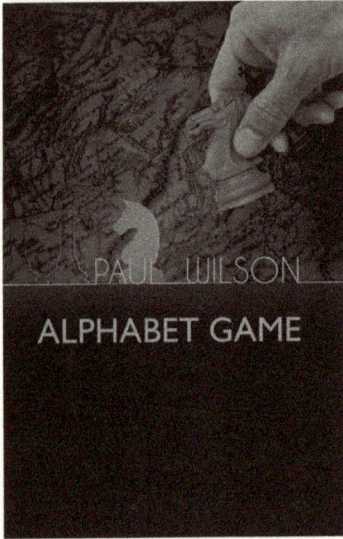

The Alphabet Game
by Paul Wilson

With the future of Guidebooks under threat, The Alphabet Game takes you back to the very beginning, back to their earliest incarnations and the gamesmanship that brought them into being. As Evelyn Waugh's Scoop did for Foreign Correspondents the world over, so this novel lifts the lid on Travel Writers for good.

Travelling around the world may appear as easy as A,B,C in the twenty first century, but looks can be deceptive: there is no 'X' for a start. Not since Xidakistan was struck from the map. But post 9/11, with the War on Terror going global, the sovereignty of 'The Valley' is back on the agenda. Could the Xidakis, like their Uzbek and Tajik neighbours, be about to taste the freedom of independence? Will Xidakistan once again take its rightful place in the League of Nations?

The Valley's fate is inextricably linked with that of Graham Ruff, founder of Ruff Guides. In a tale setting sail where Around the World in Eighty Days and Lost Horizon weighed anchor, our not-quite-a-hero suffers all the slings and arrows outrageous fortune can muster, in his pursuit of the golden triangle: The Game, The Guidebook, The Girl.

Wilson tells The Game's story with his usual mix of irreverent wit and historical insight, and in doing so delivers the most telling satire on an American war effort since M*A*S*H.

The Guidebook is Dead? Long Live the Guidebook.

RRP: £14.95
ISBN: 978-0-9927873-2-5

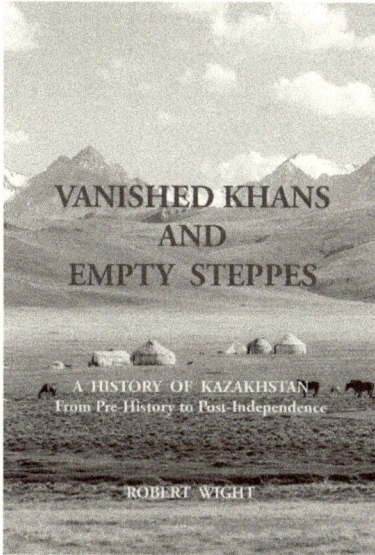

Vanished Khans and Empty Steppes
by Robert Wight

This is a major new history of an increasingly important country in Central Asia.

The book opens with an outline of the history of Almaty, from its nineteenth-century origins as a remote outpost of the Russian empire, up to its present status as the thriving second city of modern-day Kazakhstan. The story then goes back to the Neolithic and early Bronze Ages, and the sensational discovery of the famous Golden Man of the Scythian empire. A succession of armies and empires, tribes and khanates, appeared and disappeared, before the siege and destruction in 1219 of the ancient Silk Road city of Otrar under the Mongol leader Genghis Khan. The emergence of the first identifiable Kazakh state in the sixteenth century was followed by early contacts with Russia, the country which came to be the dominant influence in Kazakhstan and Central Asia for three hundred years. The book shows how Kazakhstan has been inextricably caught up in the vast historical processes – of revolution, civil war, and the rise and fall of communism - which have extended out from Russia over the last century. In the process the country has changed dramatically, from a simple nomadic society of khans and clans, to a modern and outward-looking nation. The transition has been difficult and tumultuous for millions of people, but Vanished Khans and Empty Steppes illustrates how Kazakhstan has emerged as one of the world's most successful post-communist countries.

RRP: £24.50
ISBN: 978-0-9930444-0-3

THE GODS OF THE MIDDLE WORLD
by Galina Dolgaya

The Gods of the Middle World, the new novel by Galina Dolgaya, tells the story of Sima, a student of archaeology for whom the old lore and ways of the Central Asian steppe peoples are as vivid as the present. When she joints a group of archaeologists in southern Kazakhstan, asking all the time whether it is really possible to 'commune with the spirits', she soon discovers the answer first hand, setting in motion events in the spirit worlds that have been frozen for centuries. Meanwhile three millennia earlier, on the same spot, a young woman and her companion struggle to survive and amend wrongs that have caused the neighbouring tribe to avenge for them. The two narratives mirror one another, while Sima finds her destiny intertwined with the struggle between the forces of good and evil. Drawing richly on the historical and mythical backgrounds of the southern Kazakh steppe, the novel ultimately addresses the responsibilities of each generation for those that follow and the central importance of love and forgiveness.

Based in Tashkent and with a lifetime of first-hand knowledge of the region in which the story is set, Galina Dolgaya has published a number of novels and poems in Russian. The Gods of the Middle World won first prize at the 2012 Open Central Asia Literature Festival and is her first work to be available in English, published by Hertfordshire Press.

RRP: £14.95
ISBN: 978-09574807-9-7